The Harlem Renaissance: A Very Short Introduction

VERY SHORT INTRODUCTIONS are for anyone wanting a stimulating and accessible way into a new subject. They are written by experts, and have been translated into more than 40 different languages.

The series began in 1995, and now covers a wide variety of topics in every discipline. The VSI library now contains over 450 volumes—a Very Short Introduction to everything from Indian philosophy to psychology and American history and relativity—and continues to grow in every subject area.

Very Short Introductions available now:

ACCOUNTING Christopher Nobes
ADOLESCENCE Peter K. Smith
ADVERTISING Winston Fletcher
AFRICAN AMERICAN RELIGION
    Eddie S. Glaude Jr.
AFRICAN HISTORY John Parker and
    Richard Rathbone
AFRICAN RELIGIONS Jacob K. Olupona
AGNOSTICISM Robin Le Poidevin
AGRICULTURE
    Paul Brassley and Richard Soffe
ALEXANDER THE GREAT
    Hugh Bowden
ALGEBRA Peter M. Higgins
AMERICAN HISTORY Paul S. Boyer
AMERICAN IMMIGRATION
    David A. Gerber
AMERICAN LEGAL HISTORY
    G. Edward White
AMERICAN POLITICAL
    HISTORY Donald Critchlow
AMERICAN POLITICAL PARTIES
    AND ELECTIONS L. Sandy Maisel
AMERICAN POLITICS
    Richard M. Valelly
THE AMERICAN
    PRESIDENCY Charles O. Jones
THE AMERICAN
    REVOLUTION Robert J. Allison
AMERICAN SLAVERY
    Heather Andrea Williams
THE AMERICAN WEST Stephen Aron
AMERICAN WOMEN'S HISTORY
    Susan Ware

ANAESTHESIA Aidan O'Donnell
ANARCHISM Colin Ward
ANCIENT ASSYRIA Karen Radner
ANCIENT EGYPT Ian Shaw
ANCIENT EGYPTIAN ART AND
    ARCHITECTURE Christina Riggs
ANCIENT GREECE Paul Cartledge
THE ANCIENT NEAR EAST
    Amanda H. Podany
ANCIENT PHILOSOPHY Julia Annas
ANCIENT WARFARE
    Harry Sidebottom
ANGELS David Albert Jones
ANGLICANISM Mark Chapman
THE ANGLO - SAXON AGE John Blair
THE ANIMAL KINGDOM
    Peter Holland
ANIMAL RIGHTS David DeGrazia
THE ANTARCTIC Klaus Dodds
ANTISEMITISM Steven Beller
ANXIETY Daniel Freeman and
    Jason Freeman
THE APOCRYPHAL GOSPELS
    Paul Foster
ARCHAEOLOGY Paul Bahn
ARCHITECTURE Andrew Ballantyne
ARISTOCRACY William Doyle
ARISTOTLE Jonathan Barnes
ART HISTORY Dana Arnold
ART THEORY Cynthia Freeland
ASTROBIOLOGY David C. Catling
ASTROPHYSICS James Binney
ATHEISM Julian Baggini
AUGUSTINE Henry Chadwick

Available soon:

For more information visit our website

www.oup.com/vsi/

Cheryl A. Wall

THE HARLEM RENAISSANCE

A Very Short Introduction

OXFORD
UNIVERSITY PRESS

OXFORD
UNIVERSITY PRESS

Oxford University Press is a department of the
University of Oxford. It furthers the University's objective
of excellence in research, scholarship, and education
by publishing worldwide. Oxford is a registered trade mark of Oxford
University Press in the UK and certain other countries.

Published in the United States of America by Oxford University Press
198 Madison Avenue, New York, NY 10016, United States of America

Library of Congress Cataloging-in-Publication Data
Names: Cheryl A. Wall, author.
Title: The Harlem Renaissance : very short introduction / Cheryl A. Wall.
Description: New York, NY : Oxford University Press, [2016] |
Series: Very short introductions | Includes bibliographical references and index.
Identifiers: LCCN 2015038527 | ISBN 9780199335558
(paperback : acid-free paper)
Subjects: LCSH: Harlem Renaissance. | American literature—African American
authors—History and criticism. | African American arts—New York
(State)—New York—20th century. | African Americans—New York
(State)—New York—Intellectual life. | African Americans in popular
culture. | African Americans in literature. | Harlem
(New York, N.Y.)—Intellectual life. | BISAC: LITERARY COLLECTIONS /
African. | LITERARY CRITICISM / General.
Classification: LCC PS153.N5 W327 2016 | DDC 810.9/896073—dc23 LC record
available at http://lccn.loc.gov/2015038527

1 3 5 7 9 8 6 4 2

Printed in Great Britain
by Ashford Colour Press Ltd., Gosport, Hants.
on acid-free paper

Contents

List of illustrations

Chapter 1
"When the Negro was in vogue"

The twenties were, as Langston Hughes remembered them, the period "when the Negro was in vogue" and "whites flocked to Harlem in droves." In his memoir, *The Big Sea*, Hughes offers wry descriptions of the scene: the music, dancing, and nightclubs, fancy balls and house-rent parties, and the writers, almost all of whom he knew, respected, and mentioned by name. Hughes lists Gwendolyn Bennett, Countee Cullen, Zora Neale Hurston, Nella Larsen, and Wallace Thurman among the "Harlem literati." While claiming not to have a critical mind, Hughes deems Jean Toomer "one of the most talented of the Negro writers," although Toomer did not wish to associate with Negroes. Hughes could not resist mocking the pretensions of those who "thought the race problem had at last been solved through Art plus Gladys Bentley," a reference that signified on several levels. The project of the New Negro Renaissance, as it was then called, was to achieve through art the equality that black Americans had been denied in the social, political, and economic realms. Segregation was the law in much of the United States, and the practice in the rest. Despite the creation of the National Association for the Advancement of Colored People (NAACP, founded in 1909) and the National Urban League (founded in 1910), the fight for equality had been thwarted.

But at a time when the Negro was in vogue, progress on the cultural front seemed possible. Race leaders called for the representation of Negroes as upstanding and respectable citizens. Gladys Bentley was not the emblem leaders had in mind. Usually costumed in a white tuxedo and top hat, Bentley sang and played barrelhouse blues and Tin Pan Alley tunes, whose lyrics she raunchily rewrote, in clubs that catered to a sexually adventurous clientele. The Renaissance itself was a combustible mix of the serious, the ephemeral, the aesthetic, the political, and the risqué.

It arrived on the heels of the Great War that promised to end all wars. Optimism defined the national mood, and the Renaissance reflected the particular optimism of black Americans. Black men had fought for the right to fight in the war, and having proven their patriotism on the battlefield, these veterans returned intent on claiming their citizenship rights. Their mood and the social realities they encountered did not mesh. The decade after the war saw anti-black riots, a growing number of lynchings, and the rise of the Ku Klux Klan. Yet black people mobilized and in some cases prospered. Marcus Garvey's Universal Negro Improvement Association (UNIA) preached race pride and the gospel of "Africa for the Africans," while Madame C. J. Walker became the first black woman millionaire by selling hair-straightening products. Jazz, with its syncopated rhythms and improvisations, its fusion of Tin Pan Alley and the blues, caught the contradictions that defined the age.

White Americans also embraced the music, and they learned the dances: the Charleston became the iconic dance of the twenties. Although they did not come in the "droves" that Hughes averred, a number of well-heeled whites made their way uptown to learn the moves. In a tongue-in-cheek essay titled "The Causasian Storms Harlem," Rudolph Fisher, whose dual vocation was writer/physician, describes his return to his old stomping ground after a five-year absence. Finding no familiar faces, he concludes, "the best of Harlem's black cabarets have changed their names and turned white." He notes the popularity of black art on Broadway, on the concert stage, and even in the galleries of the Metropolitan

Museum. With the wit for which he was well known, he summed up the commercial vogue: "Negro stock is going up, and everybody's buying." Or so it seemed.

We now call this era the Harlem Renaissance. It was not just a time when the Negro was in vogue, although it was certainly that; it was also a time when black people redefined themselves and announced their entrance into modernity. They responded to its opportunities and its challenges: urbanization, technology, and the disruption of traditional social arrangements and values. The Harlem Renaissance occurred against the backdrop of the Great Migration, the mass movement of black people from the rural South to northern cities that gained momentum during the First World War. Alain Locke captured the spirit of the change when he described the migration of Negroes to the city, as "a deliberate flight not only from countryside to city, but from medieval America to modern." Locke was loath to credit the economic and social factors that produced the migration; he insisted that it reflected a change in consciousness above all.

Material conditions in the South were of course a major impetus to Negro flight. Wages for blacks varied from seventy-five cents a day on farms to $1.75 for menial jobs in southern cities. By contrast, the average wage for unskilled work in the North ranged from $3.00 to $8.00 per day. Living conditions for southern blacks were abysmal; rural sharecroppers were usually housed in the cabins left standing from the time of slavery. Thus, Locke's implicit reference to southern feudalism was well founded. Sharecroppers paid the rent for the land they farmed by giving a share of the crops to the owner; they almost never raised enough to cover what they owed and soon accumulated debts beyond what they could ever pay. In effect, they were bound to land they did not own (see fig. 1). Most rural communities had no secondary schools for blacks; primary schools followed an agricultural calendar rather than an academic one, so children could be available to plant and harvest crops. And too, mob violence became a constant threat. Almost 3,000 blacks were lynched between 1885 and 1918, a period that the historian Rayford Logan deemed "the nadir for the Negro." After the 1896 *Plessy v. Ferguson* Supreme Court case decided that the doctrine of "separate but equal" was the law of the land, "Jim Crow" laws were enacted across the South. Transportation, public accommodations, and schools were lawfully segregated; facilities for "colored" were never remotely equal to those reserved for whites. To make matters worse for rural black southerners (fig. 1), floods devastated Alabama and Mississippi in 1915, and an infestation of boll weevils decimated the cotton crop.

At this same time, the war effort, responding to demands from the Allies in Europe, increased the demand for labor. The war had cut off immigration from Europe, and there were not enough white workers to fill the need, so northern employers sought out black laborers in the South. With the promise of better wages, sanitary housing, public school education for their children, and freedom

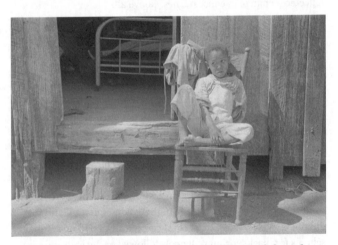

1. By the thousands, participants in the Great Migration left rural southern homes like this one: the son of a black farmer sits in front of his cabin south of Marshall, Texas.

from mob violence, black men and women traveled north. Some came alone, while others moved in families and even larger groups. Black southerners often made the journey in stages, moving from rural hamlets to southern cities, and finally to the northern hubs.

By the time they arrived, they had acquired the new consciousness that Locke celebrated. It had taken courage to move, and it required grit to stay in places that in no way resembled home. Like the European immigrants who had earlier landed in waves in northern cities, black migrants struggled to adapt to the pace of urban life, its sense of dislocation, and anonymity. Although some struggled to hold on to their old ways—their religious and social rituals—others were thrilled to leave old rituals and mores behind. Absent the monotonous routines of rural life, the prying eyes of small-town neighbors, and the expectation that one would follow in one's parents' footsteps, many newcomers felt free to reinvent themselves.

Although the term "New Negro" was associated with the elite, workers also rejected the racist stereotypes that depicted blacks as servile and submissive, traits that were captured under the sign "Old Negro." They too assumed a stance of autonomy and pride. But it was the elite that produced the social and cultural upsurge. As Langston Hughes observed, "ordinary Negroes hadn't heard of the Negro Renaissance. And if they had, it hadn't raised their wages any." Nevertheless, the art of those ordinary Negroes—their dance, speech, songs, and stories—would become the motive forces of the cultural awakening, the New Negro Renaissance that engaged poets and novelists, musicians, painters and sculptors, and theatrical performers during the 1920s and 1930s. Blues and jazz, folk idioms, and urban vernacular would become the building blocks of black modernism.

It is impossible to pinpoint the exact moment the awakening began. Many historians identify its beginning with the end of World War I, when black enlisted men came marching home expecting to find the democracy for which they had fought overseas, but there are several origin stories. Langston Hughes chose the opening of *Shuffle Along*, the 1921 show written by Flournoy Miller and Aubrey Lyles, with music by Eubie Blake and Noble Sissle, and performances by Josephine Baker, Adelaide Hall, and Florence Mills. A veritable sensation as well as the first musical revue to include a plot, it introduced the popular songs, "Love Will Find a Way" and "I'm Just Wild About Harry." Literary scholars point to the 1919 publication of Claude McKay's searing sonnet, "If We Must Die," or the publication of James Weldon Johnson's anthology, *The Book of American Negro Poetry* in 1922, or Jean Toomer's *Cane* in 1923. Each of these signaled a new moment in African American literary history. McKay's poem declared the Negro's right to self-defense in a form that led the reviewer Jessie Fauset to exclaim, "*This is poetry!*" In his preface, Weldon Johnson argued that "the final measure of the greatness of all peoples is the amount and standard of the literature and art they have produced," which might have provoked Hughes's riposte about art and Gladys Bentley. Nonetheless, the anthology's value derived both from the poetry it collected and from the preface that defined art broadly enough to include spirituals, folklore, the cakewalk, and ragtime. If the last were updated as popular dance and jazz, these four entities were the forms that inspired much of the art of the Harlem Renaissance. The genius of *Cane* was Toomer's ability to fuse folk traditions (such as spirituals and work songs) with the innovations of Anglo-American modernism. As important as any of these specific cultural texts were, however, none could be said to be *the* originary moment.

The year the Renaissance ended is equally in dispute. Some historians identify 1929 and the financial collapse as the end point. The Depression dashed much of the optimism that had characterized black life in the 1920s. The promise of Harlem as a self-sufficient community faded as did the uptown jaunts of rich white visitors. But if the onset of the Depression ended the vogue for Harlem, it did not signal the end of the Renaissance. More books by black writers were published during the 1930s than in the 1920s. Arguably, the riot that devastated Harlem in 1935 marked the end of the Renaissance. It sealed Harlem's transformation from "promised land" to ghetto, a designation it carried for the rest of the century.

Periodization is at best a literary fiction. Scholars write the history of all literary periods retrospectively; as they do, they typically exclude the female participants in any movement. In this case, if one were to agree that the Renaissance ended in 1929 or even 1935, one would exclude all but one of Zora Neale Hurston's novels, including *Their Eyes Were Watching God*, published in 1937. More than a vogue, the Harlem Renaissance was the most influential period in African American literary history before the last quarter of the twentieth century. In its most expansive and most useful conception, it spans the decades between the two world wars. As World War II began, Richard Wright and other black writers set a very different tone from their precursors.

If it is difficult to pinpoint beginnings and endings, it is just as easy to choose key moments and figures that evoke both the spirit of the time and the substance of its achievement. To cite several:

On March 21, 1924, an elegant dinner took place at the Civic Club, perhaps the fanciest venue in Manhattan that welcomed an integrated clientele. Its host was Charles S. Johnson, a sociologist, who served as the editor of *Opportunity* magazine, the official publication of the Urban League. It was, as he later described it, the "debut of the younger school of Negro writers." Most of them attended, including the poets Gwendolyn Bennett, Countee Cullen, and Langston Hughes, the fiction writer Eric Walrond, and Walter White, a NAACP official and soon-to-be-published novelist. They were joined by their elders: W. E. B. Du Bois, the founding editor of *The Crisis, A Record of the Darker Races*, the official publication of the NAACP; James Weldon Johnson; and the poet Georgia Douglas Johnson. These black luminaries were presented to an audience that included the heads of major publishing houses—Harper Brothers, Boni and Liveright, and Scribners—as well as editors of influential mainstream journals—the *Century*, the *World Tomorrow*, the *Nation*, and *Survey Graphic*. Among the white authors attending were the playwrights Eugene O'Neill (*The Emperor Jones* and *All God's Chillun Got Wings*) and Ridgely Torrence (*Granny Maumee* and *Simon the Cyrenian*), whose work had won favor with black audiences and opened opportunities for black actors. The novelist T. S. Stribling also attended. Jessie Fauset had written that his *Birthright* had inspired her to write a novel, "to tell the truth about us," more honestly than Stribling, despite his good intentions, had been able to do. The literary editor of the *Crisis*, a poet, and a translator, Fauset had achieved success with her first novel, *There Is Confusion* (1923); she was told the dinner was in her honor. It was not.

It was instead the official launch of the Renaissance. Soon afterward, the evening's master of ceremonies, Alain Locke, a Harvard PhD, a Rhodes scholar, and philosophy professor at Howard University, was asked to edit a special issue of *Survey Graphic*, a social work magazine. The issue became the kernel of *The New Negro* (1925), the signal anthology of the Renaissance that collected essays, short stories, and poems. With essays on "The Drama of Negro Life," "The Negro Spirituals," "Jazz at Home," and "The Legacy of the Ancestral Arts," it defines a multifaceted cultural movement that includes music, theater, and visual art as well as literature. Not only were almost all of the New Negro writers included but also most of the leading Negro intellectuals and scholars. Social scientists contributed articles on the Great Migration, Negro education, and business. Several of the pieces, notably W. A. Domingo's "Gift of the Black Tropics" and Du Bois's "Worlds of Color," expanded the scope of the movement beyond the borders of the United States. The volume also included pieces by progressive white scholars and writers, including Arthur Barnes (later to earn renown as the founder of the Barnes Foundation), Montgomery Gregory, Melville Herskovits, and Paul Kellogg.

Countee Cullen was one of the young writers from whom much was expected. The adopted son of the Reverend and Mrs. Frederick Cullen, he had grown up in the parsonage of Salem Methodist Church, one of Harlem's largest congregations. The spiritual themes and biblical allusions in his poetry bore traces of his upbringing. Cullen's first poem won notice in his own right, when the *New York Times* noted his achievement as a poet at DeWitt Clinton High School. By the time he graduated from New York University in 1925, he had published in *Harper's*, the *Crisis*, and *Opportunity*, and his first volume of poems, *Color*, was in press. It more than met the expectations of his eager public with poems such as "Heritage," "Incident," and "Yet Do I Marvel," a sonnet that summed up the paradoxical situation of a poet who believed with his favorite poet John Keats that "beauty is truth and truth is beauty," but Cullen also felt a keen obligation to depict the often ugly realities of life for his fellow black Americans. The sonnet's final couplet stated his determination to persist: "Yet do I marvel at this curious thing / To make a poet black and bid him sing!"

In 1925 Cullen was the most famous black American poet, but he had already lost a poetry competition to Langston Hughes, whose fame would be more enduring. Born in Joplin, Missouri, in 1902, Hughes grew up with his grandmother, Mary Langston, in Lawrence, Kansas; Mary Langston's late husband had ridden with John Brown at Harpers Ferry. Langston later moved with his mother to Cleveland, where he finished high school. His father, so embittered by racism in the United States that he moved to Mexico, wanted his son to train as a mining engineer. But Hughes knew early on that writing was his vocation; when he was nineteen he wrote the classic poem, "The Negro Speaks of Rivers," as he rode a train home from Mexico after visiting his father. Still, he pretended to accept his father's plan and persuaded him to pay his tuition to Columbia, not because he wanted to attend the Ivy League university but because "more than Paris, or the Shakespeare country, or Berlin or the Alps, I wanted to see Harlem, the greatest Negro city in the world." Harlem became not only his home but also a wellspring of poetic inspiration.

"The Weary Blues," the title poem of Hughes's first book, merits closer consideration. The poem pens a portrait of a black man playing the piano in a bar on Lenox Avenue, in the kind of neighborhood hangout frequented by those who had not heard of the Renaissance. Although the song he sings was traditional among rural African Americans, the music and the setting were new for poetry in 1926. Paul Laurence Dunbar had initiated a school of dialect poetry at the turn of the twentieth century, but no one before Hughes had treated the blues as a subject and source for formal poetry. Hughes interpolates a folk lyric: "I've got the weary blues and can't be satisfied / I've got the weary blues and can't be satisfied / I ain't happy no mo' and wish that I had died," which he had heard while growing up in Kansas. Also titled "The Weary Blues," the folk lyric itself is framed by Hughes's own blues-inflected lines. The poem does not specify the man's circumstances, but with poetic indirection it defines the spirit and the sound of the blues: "a syncopated tune," "a mellow croon," "sad raggy tune," "melancholy tone," all "coming from a black man's soul." If the spirit partakes of the popular understanding of the blues as a state of mind, the syncopated, mellow, and raggy (after ragtime) sound evokes the music and suggests how generative it could be for poetry. Finally, "The Weary Blues" enacts the process through which blues offered a release from pain. After experiencing what the Greeks termed *catharsis*, the man whom the poem depicts as playing through the night "sleeps like a rock / or a man that's dead." Having sung his way through his trouble, he achieves physical and psychic release. Although we do not learn much about him, we know that this man is not a rural subject. He may know the folk blues from an earlier life, but for now he is totally at home in Harlem.

Several key figures missed the Civic Club party. Claude McKay spent most of the Renaissance traveling the world—London, Marseilles, Moscow, and Tangiers were among his ports of call. Born in Jamaica in 1889, he started writing poetry in the local vernacular while working as a constable. In 1912 he published two volumes, *Constab Ballads* and *Songs of Jamaica*; and that same year he left his birthplace, never to return. In the United States, he was first a student then a worker, whose jobs included porter, bar-boy, houseman, and railroad dining-car waiter. These experiences were transformative, for, as McKay reflected, "It was not until I was forced now among the rough body of the great service class of Negroes that I got to know my AfraAmerica." For that reason, *his* black America was different from that of his bourgeois peers. He lived in Harlem for a time but left for England in 1919, just having achieved his first literary success. A self-proclaimed radical, McKay allied himself with the leftist community in New York; that affiliation led to the publication of his first poems in the United States, appearing in *Seven Arts* and *The Liberator*. The poem "If We Must Die" was written in response to the Red Summer of 1919, when anti-black riots broke out across the country in cities as far apart as Chicago, Washington, and Elaine, Arkansas. Mobs of white men often rampaged through Negro neighborhoods, as they sought to restore the racial status quo that the war had slightly shifted. "If We Must Die" channeled the spirit of the New Negro, who resisted these attacks. A novelist as well as a poet, McKay would write the only bestseller by a black author of the era, *Home to Harlem*, in 1928.

Nella Larsen missed the dinner as well, although she was known to frequent the Civic Club. In the 1920s she divided her time between Uptown Manhattan and Greenwich Village. She never felt completely at home in Harlem, yet she lived there during its heyday. She published two well-regarded novels, *Quicksand* (1928) and *Passing* (1929), and not long afterward, she disappeared from Harlem and from literature. She had been an outsider all her life. Born in Chicago in 1891, she was the daughter of a white mother, a Danish immigrant, and a black father, who emigrated from the Danish (now the U.S.) Virgin Islands. Her father died when she was an infant; her mother remarried a white Danish immigrant who detested his wife's biracial daughter. Larsen was keenly aware of the pain her presence caused her mother. After graduating from high school, and with her mother's help, she enrolled at Fisk University in Nashville. Here, for the first time, she was in an all-Negro environment, but it proved no more satisfying. An indifferent student, she chafed at the rigid codes of conduct and was expelled after her first year. She then traveled to Denmark, where she came of age in a country where she was both stranger and kin.

On her return to the United States in 1912, Larsen enrolled in nursing school at Lincoln Hospital and Home in the Bronx. The program was specifically for Negro students, even though many of the patients they cared for were white. After graduation, she took a job as head nurse at the hospital of Tuskegee Institute, founded by the formidable Booker T. Washington. The work was exhausting, and the atmosphere proved stultifying. Off campus, segregation was strictly enforced, while on campus, faculty and staff were subject to the same strict rules as students: strict curfews and mandatory chapel.

Larsen returned to New York, signed on as a public health nurse, and met and married Elmer Imes, a research physicist with a doctorate from the University of Michigan. He came from a prominent Negro family and enjoyed the arts as much as Larsen did. The attractive couple led a glamorous social life. Larsen began volunteering at the 135th Street Library, the foremost cultural center in Harlem, and perhaps the time she spent there motivated her to shift careers. She graduated from the New York Public Library School—she was its first Negro graduate—and eventually took a position at the 135th Street branch. In addition to staffing the children's room, she planned readings, lectures, and exhibitions. Then she decided that she wanted to create art rather than simply present it. Her fiction would, as she hoped, catch the panorama of its time, at least as life was lived in its more cosmopolitan precincts.

Jean Toomer was not at the Civic Club dinner either, but his publisher, Charles Boni, rose to lament the poor sales that *Cane* had achieved in its first year of publication. Toomer's peers, if not the reading public, knew how important *Cane* was. A mélange of poems, sketches, short stories, and a novella, the book paints a broad canvas of Negro life in the 1920s. Deploying modernist techniques such as free verse, imagism, and stream-of consciousness, it conveys the alienation of urban life, the beauty of the southern landscape, and the stunted lives of the blacks who inhabit it. Toomer had been inspired by his sojourn in Sparta, Georgia, in 1921. There, he reflected, "I received my initial impulse to an individual art.... For no other section of the country as so stirred me. There one finds soil, soil in the sense the Russians know it—the soil every art and literature that is to live must be imbedded in."

Born in Washington, D.C., Toomer had lived his life in cities, chiefly Washington, New York, and Chicago. He was the grandson of P. B. S. Pinchback, who had served as the governor of Louisiana during Reconstruction. The family's fortunes had declined, and his parents' failed marriage left Toomer with uncertain prospects. He studied at several institutions, including the University of Chicago and the University of Wisconsin as well as the American College of Physical Training in Chicago, before he found his voice as a writer. Then, in 1922, Jessie Fauset accepted two of his poems for the *Crisis*. She praised his work extravagantly but cautioned that he was "a little inclined to achieve style at the expense of clearness."

Never at home in Harlem, Toomer spent much of his time in Manhattan's Greenwich Village, where he befriended the writers

Sherwood Anderson and Waldo Frank. He became an adherent of George Gurdjieff, the Russian mystic whose teachings appealed to members of the artistic avant-garde. At this point, Toomer tried with little success to recruit converts in Harlem. Increasingly unhappy with racial classifications, he began to identify himself as simply "American." Although his work had been included in Weldon Johnson's anthology and would appear in *The New Negro*, Toomer stopped granting permission for his work to appear in anthologies of black writing. He would eventually leave the Negro world behind, but *Cane* would influence generations of black writers.

Zora Neale Hurston arrived in New York in January 1925, too late for the "official" launch of the Renaissance. She wasted no time in meeting the right people. Within months, she was awarded the second place prize for drama at an awards dinner sponsored by *Opportunity* magazine. She took the stage, scarf flowing, and intoned the name of her play, "*COLOR. . R.R. STRUCK. . K.K.*!" As Hurston was quick to tell anyone who asked, she was from the all-black town of Eatonville, Florida, which provided the setting for *Color Struck* and much of her subsequent fiction. Hurston's southern roots gave her something in common with most Harlemites but not with the Negro literati, or, as she preferred, "niggerati." Few of them were from the South. At the *Opportunity* dinner, Hurston met Annie Nathan Meyer, a Barnard alumna, who arranged for Hurston to matriculate at the school. At Barnard, Hurston came under the influence of the pioneering American anthropologist, Franz Boas, who gave her the tools to study the folklore that she carried as her birthright. Armed with what she called "the spyglass of Anthropology," she spent much of the Renaissance on the road, crisscrossing the South collecting the tales, songs, sermons, children's games, and hoodoo rituals that she published in *Mules and Men*, the first volume of African American folklore collected by an African American, in 1935.

Mules and Men was the product of Hurston's brilliant intellect, scholarly training, and personal courage. Yet she could not have conducted her research without the financial support of a patron. Few Americans, white or black, believed in the value of Negro folklore, and few even thought that art created by black people was important. In order to produce their work, several artists relied on rich individuals who supported them while they completed their projects. The politics of patronage was vexed, or as Hurston described her relationship with her patron, Charlotte Osgood Mason, "curious." Hurston insisted that a "psychic bond" existed between the two, which allowed each woman to read the other's thoughts. "Godmother," she declared in her autobiography, *Dust Tracks on a Road*, "was just as pagan as I." Psychic bonds notwithstanding, Hurston and Mason signed a contract, the terms of which designated Hurston as Mason's agent who would collect Negro folklore on Mason's behalf. Mason would "own" the material. In return, Hurston was given a car and a camera, and she was paid a stipend of $200 a month from 1927 until 1932. She had to account for every dime; her ledger lists expenditures for everything from memberships in professional organizations to intimate personal items.

Unlike the relationship between the holder of a fellowship and a foundation, that between artist and patron is highly personal, inherently unequal, and, for Harlem Renaissance artists, disfigured by primitivist and racialist myths. Alain Locke, the forty-year-old professor whom Mason referred to as her "precious brown boy," had introduced Hurston to Mason. Having exhausted her previous preoccupation with the Indians of the Southwest, Mason then discovered the Negro. She projected her ideas of the primitive onto the well-educated, sophisticated artists who sought her support. Locke was the go-between who shepherded Langston Hughes, the sculptor Richmond Barthé, and the composer Hall Johnson to Mason's Park Avenue apartment. For varying lengths of time, all of these men depended on Mason's largess. In the main, they were able to negotiate the challenge of meeting her expectations without compromising their artistic and personal integrity.

Musicians faced challenges too, but attracting audiences was not one of them. On December 4, 1927, Duke Ellington and his orchestra began a career-making run at the Cotton Club, the legendary nightspot at 142nd Street and Lenox Avenue, where blacks were welcomed only as waiters and performers. Ellington's orchestra had made records for a string of labels, but its first hit was the newly waxed "Creole Love Call," with the wordless vocals of Adelaide Hall. The record became an international sensation. By then Ellington, or his manager, was already in negotiation with the owner of the Cotton Club. Ellington had not been the owner's first choice, but New Orleans's King Oliver had declined an offer to front the club's house band. Ellington quickly accepted and added five more players to his six-piece group that had named themselves the Washingtonians after their hometown. The new ensemble—with players including trumpeter Bubber Miley, trombonist Tricky Sam Nanton, and drummer Buddy Greer—accompanied the club's vaudeville acts and provided musical interludes. Ellington eventually created a revue called "Rhythmania," that featured Hall. With the Cotton Club gig, the Duke Ellington Orchestra had hit the big time. Despite, or perhaps because of, its underworld connections, the Cotton Club attracted a wealthy, celebrity-laden clientele. Whites came to Harlem, their pleasure fueled by illicit liquor and the *frisson* of interracial encounter. Handsome and charismatic, Ellington was a musical prodigy and a natural-born aristocrat. He and his band were as elegantly attired as any of the club's patrons (fig. 2).

Whether the fancy clothes and the reasonably generous pay actually compensated for the segregated arrangements, the gig allowed Ellington's music to reach an audience over the airwaves that could not be limited by race or class. Radio was a new medium that gave Americans access to entertainment on a theretofore unimaginable scale. Ellington's was the first African American band to gain national exposure. Broadcasting live from the Cotton Club on Monday nights—either at midnight or at 6 p.m., the latter in a "supper time" slot—the orchestra created legions of fans who

2. **Bandleader Duke Ellington (seated at piano) and his orchestra perform at the world-famous Cotton Club in Harlem in 1931. The band's radio broadcasts from the nightspot popularized jazz in the 1920s.**

experienced music unlike any that they had heard. With these broadcasts, the Jazz Age, as F. Scott Fitzgerald dubbed the decade, was in full swing. Ellington brought jazz into the homes of Americans who could never have had the opportunity to visit any nightspot, let alone the famous Cotton Club.

The club's décor juxtaposed images of the plantation South and the African "jungle." Ellington's recordings were marketed as "jungle music," a rubric that reinforced the fantasies promoted by the club owners. Records like "Echoes of the Jungle" and "Jungle Nights in Harlem" featured "pseudo-African" musical effects, including tom toms, unusual harmonies, and growling trumpets and trombones, none of which could be traced to Africa but which produced highly danceable music. Ellington understood his musical identity and its importance, as his insistence on the title "orchestra" signified. "Black Beauty," composed in honor of the musical comedy star, Florence Mills, spoke to Ellington's race consciousness. But against a backdrop of faux jungles and cotton fields, the possibilities for confusion were limitless. Some whites fantasized an encounter with "primitives," while some blacks imagined themselves *as* "primitives," even though almost all were Americans in twentieth-century New York.

Josephine Baker's international career unfolded against a similar backdrop; racial mythologies had taken root across the Western world by the 1920s. A dancer and comedienne, Baker had a small role in *Shuffle Along*, but with her antics she often stole the show. The run was a huge success, but it did not make Baker a star: it took *Le Revue Nègre* to accomplish that. Arriving in Paris in 1925, the show, which featured jazzman Sidney Bechet along with a cast of veteran vaudeville performers, took the city by storm. By the following year, according to *Vanity Fair*, Josephine Baker and Woodrow Wilson were the two best-known Americans in postwar Europe. To Europeans, Baker embodied the exotic primitive. One commonplace held that "Baker dancing looked like an African sculpture come to life." Finding her dance "a wild splendor and magnificent animality," an eminent critic concluded that the effect of her performance ("the frenzy of African Eros swept over the audience") was akin to that of the black Venus that haunted Baudelaire. In truth, her dance styles were totally made-in-America. Yet when she performed the Charleston, bare-breasted and girdled by her infamous banana skirt, her European audiences saw in her a colonialist's fantasy.

While Baker enjoyed the epithet "Black Venus" and used it frequently to refer to herself, she was well aware that she was not what her audiences believed her to be. Her comedic talent enabled her to mock the image with a wink and a roll of the eye. She played the part on and off stage, strolling down the Champs Élysées with a pet leopard. When a reporter told Baker that she symbolized primitivism, she was incredulous: "What are you trying to say? I was born in 1906 in the twentieth century." Baker did seem to want to have it both ways. Not only did she adorn her half-naked body with feathers and dangling jewelry, she danced with the suggestiveness that fulfilled her audience's erotic fantasies about black women. Still, she withheld something of herself and responded fiercely to those who confused her with her role. On the streets of Harlem, Baker's fans did not fault her for conforming to any stereotype. They reveled in her theatrical triumph and her commercial success: her image sold dolls, costumes, perfumes, and pomades. The news that Parisian women wore their hair slicked down, à la Baker's—that some even purchased a product called Bakerfix to affect the look—was thrilling to ordinary black American women who had never heard of a black woman whose look white women wanted to emulate.

Black intellectuals, including W. E. B. Du Bois and Carter G. Woodson, the founder of Negro History Week, had long been concerned about the persistence of falsehoods and myths about black people, myths that as the Baker phenomenon confirmed, circulated not just in the United States but around the world. Far from the headlines in 1926, Arthur Schomburg, a Puerto Rican–born bibliophile, sold his collection of books, manuscripts, prints, photographs, and memorabilia documenting the history and culture of people of African descent to the New York Public Library. Ernestine Rose, the white woman who headed the 135th Street branch, facilitated the purchase. Schomburg, who worked in the mailroom at Bankers Trust, received $10,000 from the sale; he was then hired as the curator of his collection to be housed at the library, where it would grow into the leading research center that it is today. In 1926 the 135th Street Library was already a popular meeting place for artists and intellectuals. Schomburg had previously invited writers, including Du Bois, to use the collection for their research so that the public at large had access to it. Ordinary readers could now join in Schomburg's quest to document the history of the race.

According to an often repeated account, Schomburg's impetus for collecting was an encounter with his fifth-grade teacher who had told him that black people had no history. He spent his life refuting the lie. In his essay "The Negro Digs Up His Past," published in the *New Negro*, Schomburg wrote, "though it is orthodox to think of America as the one country where it is unnecessary to have a past, what is a luxury for the nation as a whole becomes a prime social necessity for the Negro." The metaphor of the essay's title suggests the difficulty of retrieving the past, and the reference to the American ethos suggests how unpopular the undertaking would be, but the dividends were great indeed. Blacks would learn that they had always collaborated in the struggle for their freedom. They would reject the practice of celebrating those blacks of accomplishment as "exceptions" rather than part of the group, and they would understand the contributions of people of African descent to human history. In so doing they were able to transform their understanding of themselves.

The word "Negro" was a badge of pride for Schomburg's generation. In fact, W. E. B. Du Bois had led a campaign to persuade the *New York Times* to capitalize the word. In the 1960s, "Negro" became associated with the spirit of accommodation it was intended to displace. That was the decade in which historians began their research on the cultural awakening; not surprisingly they preferred the then less controversial term "Harlem Renaissance." And that was the term that has stuck. Its persistence is striking, given the fact that as early as the 1920s, Sterling Brown, a poet and pioneering literary scholar, insisted that there was no such thing as a "Harlem Renaissance." Although Brown spent most of his life on the faculty of Howard University in Washington, D.C., many other writers whose names were associated with the Renaissance never lived in Harlem. While Harlem remained a key location then, the Harlem Renaissance that this book introduces reaches across the nation and the globe.

Black people in cities across the world responded to a common impetus to view themselves as modern subjects. They met and produced journals and exhibitions in Boston, Philadelphia, and Washington, all of which lay claim to our attention. In Boston, the conservative influence of the poet and critic William Stanley Braithwaite was evident even in the title of its publication, *The Quill*. In Philadelphia, a small group published *Black Opals*, a literary journal. In Washington, the poet Georgia Douglas Johnson hosted a salon, the "Saturday Nighters," which not only provided a meeting place for the black literati of D.C. but also welcomed writers from outside the city. Arguably, Chicago boasted the most vibrant jazz scene; there Louis Armstrong became a major and important creative force. As scholars have more recently demonstrated, the development of black modernism was a transatlantic phenomenon, and Paris, no less than Harlem, was a crucial site. Yet, the names alone of none of these other cities evoke the cultural specificity of Harlem. We can speak of *Paris Noir*, Colored Philadelphia, and the Southside of Chicago, but Harlem signifies all by itself.

For those who had only heard about it, Harlem became in the folklore of the time "the promised land." For those who had only read about, it signified a kind of dreamscape. Léopold Senghor, along with other writers from Africa and the Caribbean, wrote poems about Harlem. There is still much to consider "beyond Harlem," as the conclusion of this book attests. But first, we need to attend to the New Negroes and their effort to rescue the race, and themselves, from the stereotypes and caricatures that represented black Americans to most of the world in the first decades of the twentieth century.

Chapter 2
Inventing new selves

Writing that "the day of 'aunties,' 'uncles,' and 'mammies' is gone," and that "Uncle Tom" and "Sambo" have passed, Alain Locke announced the advent of the "New Negro" in 1925. Sixty years after their physical emancipation, Locke declared black Americans "spiritually emancipated." They had shaken off the stereotypes that the epithets defined. These stereotypes had never defined black people; legacies of slavery, they signified more myth than man, more formula than human being. They were the caricatures that circulated throughout popular culture in the advertisements, minstrel shows, movies, and literature. They were figments of white Americans' imaginations. By contrast, New Negroes proudly defined themselves. Locke's *The New Negro* anthology was their manifesto: it aimed "to register the transformation of the inner and outer life of the Negro in America that have so significantly taken place in the last few years."

That transformation had in fact been longer in the making, and the term "New Negro" was a familiar reference. In 1900 Booker T. Washington edited *A New Negro for a New Century*, a hefty if eclectic volume that documented the heroic participation of blacks in American wars from the Revolution to the recently concluded Spanish-American conflict. It included historical essays on slavery and the Underground Railroad and ended with two essays on Negro club women. Heroism whether in the service of the nation or of the liberation of the race was a key marker of progress. The volume included more than fifty photographs of race leaders, professional men and their wives, and a handful of female educators and women devoted to racial uplift.

Booker T. Washington stood above them all. His aptly-titled autobiography *Up From Slavery*, also published in 1900, chronicled an amazing life. Born into slavery in West Virginia, he was educated at Hampton Institute, a school dedicated to vocational training and the gospel of self-help. Upon graduation, Washington was hired to found a school with a similar philosophy in Tuskegee, Alabama. A powerful orator and skilled negotiator, he won the backing of powerful white capitalists, including Andrew Carnegie and Julius Rosenwald, a founder of Sears and Roebuck and, perhaps more importantly, the philanthropic Rosenwald Fund. Soon, in addition to garnering funds for his own institution, Booker T. Washington was setting the educational agenda for black people throughout the South.

His debut on the national stage took place at the Atlanta Exposition in 1895. His speech, which W. E. B. Du Bois dubbed the "Atlanta Compromise," promised southern whites that blacks would forgo civil rights in exchange for work: "In all things purely social we can be as separate as the fingers, yet one as the hand in all things essential to mutual progress." With this metaphor Washington accepted the social segregation of Jim Crow; later in the speech he put the quest for voting rights for blacks on indefinite hold. This was his public stance, but behind the scenes he advocated for an end to the violence blacks endured, all the while seeking also to protect his position of influence.

Although Du Bois initially praised Washington's speech, he soon repudiated Washington's leadership and rebutted his philosophy. Du Bois argued political equality could not be sacrificed for material gain, even as he highlighted the extreme poverty that most black Americans continued to endure under Washington's leadership. A professor at Atlanta University, educated at Fisk, Harvard (from which he held a doctorate) and the University of Berlin, Du Bois took personal exception to Washington's dismissal of the value of liberal arts education. While a college education might be beyond the grasp of the majority, a fraction of blacks, a "talented tenth" in his phrase, could seize the opportunities it provided. Finally, he averred, enslaved people had in their religion and music expressed the human spirit more profoundly than had their white compatriots.

Du Bois distilled his ideas in *The Souls of Black Folk* (1903), a book that became a touchstone for New Negro thought. Beginning with James Weldon Johnson's *The Autobiography of an Ex-Colored Man*, novelists and poets appropriated its themes and tropes. Yet younger writers and activists chafed at the slow rate of progress for the race.

In *The New Negro: His Political, Civil, and Mental Status and Related Essays* published in 1916, William Pickens took a more adversarial stance. He protested the failure of the nation to guarantee the rights for which Negro veterans had fought in World War I. While most black Americans remained loyal patriots, Pickens implied that might not always be the case. He lamented the chasm that existed between whites and blacks. While whites longed nostalgically for the "old Negro" and feared his successor, middle-class blacks wanted the respect of their white peers.

A. Philip Randolph and Chandler Owen, the editors of the socialist journal *The Messenger*, ramped up the rhetoric and specified the demands in an essay titled "The New Negro—What Is He?" published in 1920. Their aims were political, economic, and social. Politically, they rejected patronage and called for universal suffrage. They urged blacks to repudiate both existing parties and support a party dedicated to the working class. Economically, Randolph and Owen defined the Negro as a worker whose immediate aims were better wages, shorter hours, and improved working conditions. To achieve these aims, Randolph, who would go on to found the Brotherhood of Sleeping Car Porters, urged blacks to form unions as he did. Randolph and Owen insisted on social equality for blacks and supported intermarriage. They not only supported education but endorsed self-defense. With reason, they described their aims as "radical."

Claude McKay's sonnet "If We Must Die" bristles with the spirit of their essay.

> If we must die, let it not be like hogs
> Hunted and penned in an inglorious spot,
> While round us bark the mad and hungry dogs,
> Making their mock at our accursed lot.
> If we must die, O let us nobly die,
> So that our precious blood may not be shed
> In vain; then even the monsters we defy
> Shall be constrained to honor us though dead!
> O kinsmen! we must meet the common foe!
> Though far outnumbered let us show us brave,
> And for their thousand blows deal one death-blow!
> What though before us lies the open grave?
> Like men we'll face the murderous, cowardly pack,
> Pressed to the wall, dying, but fighting back!

The sonnet makes self-defense a measure of manhood. By defending themselves against the odds, Negro men achieve the nobility that their enemies cannot attain. Indeed, rejecting the stereotypes of black people as less than human, the sonnet figures their white oppressors as dogs and monsters. The poem's diction reinforces the call to nobility; it belongs to an earlier era— "accursed," "foe," "kinsmen," "death-blow"—in which the noble acts the poem invokes were considered more common. Its use of the Shakespearean sonnet form would seem to remove the poem even farther from the present. However, the poem had an immediate impact on New Negroes. They embraced it as a statement of their determination to resist oppression.

Alain Locke was no radical. While he rejected the reliance on philanthropy associated with Booker Washington, he did not maintain Du Bois's focus on civil rights. His essays do not propose political strategies or economic policies; neither do they make political demands. The terrain on which they wage the struggle for equality is cultural. Randolph and Owens notwithstanding, black Americans had no chance of achieving political, economic, or social equality in the 1920s. The fact that the Supreme Court did not declare intermarriage legal until 1967, in the *Loving v. Virginia* decision, is just one indication of how distant the socialist vision was. But the cultural door was at least slightly ajar. Locke, along with Charles S. Johnson, James Weldon Johnson, and Jessie Fauset hoped to wedge it open. In Locke's view, the young artists who had produced "the first fruits of the Negro Renaissance" were harbingers of the future, for "the especially cultural recognition they win should in turn prove the key to that revaluation of the Negro which must precede or accompany any considerable further betterment of race relationships." Although this perspective proved utopian as well, it was at the time a source of inspiration as well as a burden to most of the movement's artists.

It is significant that Locke emphasized the new "psychology" of the younger generation. He argued that individuals were defining new identities for themselves, though he was silent on factors of identity that were not based on race. At the same time, he proposed that art serve a social function by provoking a "revaluation" of the race. He did not address the inherent tension between the creation of art and the struggle for racial progress, but that tension simmered just beneath the surface.

Negro artists were, in the main, happy to advance the cause. The "poetry of protest" became a central feature of the Renaissance. Some poems were as angry as McKay's sonnets. Others spoke in sorrowful tones: "We shall not always plant while others reap" began Countee Cullen's "From the Dark Tower." His sonnet— Petrarchan rather than Shakespearean in form—lyrically alludes to the oppression of blacks in his first stanza, which ends "We were not made eternally to weep." The second stanza begins with an image that occurs in many Harlem Renaissance poems—the identification of black people with night and an insistence on the beauty of both: "The night whose sable breast relieves the stark / White stars is no less lovely being dark." The speaker does not doubt Negroes' right to equality, but, as the final lines reveal, he has no confidence that it will be achieved: "So in the dark we hide the heart that bleeds, / And wait and tend our agonizing seeds." Cullen was a reluctant protester. Nevertheless, as he explained to a *New York Times* reporter in 1927, "In spite of myself I find that I am actutated by a strong sense of race consciousness. This grows upon me, I find, as I grow older, and although I struggle against it, it colors my writing, I fear, in spite of everything I can do."

Langston Hughes, by contrast, embraced his role as race man. His poetic influences were not English romantic poets but the Americans Walt Whitman and Carl Sandburg. As they did, Hughes had a profound faith in common people and believed their experiences and their language should be the stuff of poetry. His poems chronicle the lives of working people from the loving woman who urges her son to keep climbing in "Mother to Son" to the fun-loving Susanna Jones in "When Sue Wears Red" to the storefront congregation in "Fire" to the womanizing subject of "Sylvester's Dying Bed." The celebration of these lives is an act of protest in itself. But Hughes also confronted what he called the "American Heartache" explicitly in poems such as "Daybreak in Alabama," "Ku Klux," and "Song for a Dark Girl," a ballad about a lynching. In "I Too," he celebrates his subject's quiet heroism:

I, too, sing America
I am the darker brother.
They send me to eat in the kitchen

When company comes,
But I laugh,
And eat well,
And grow strong.

The poem enacts the transition from the Old Negro to the New Negro and represents it as a psychological transformation encoded in the shift from "I, too sing America" in the first line to "I, too, am America" in the last. The first line calls to mind Whitman's "I Hear America Singing," but this speaker cannot truly "sing" America until his identity as an American is recognized. The "I" of Hughes's poem is also a collective "I." In the present he exists in domestic relation to "America," as he is both brother and servant, though only the latter relation is acknowledged. The speaker is required to act deferentially; he eats in the kitchen when company comes, as if when there is no company his true identity is visible. Yet the effort to deny him only makes him stronger. His faith in the future is unshakeable. The word "tomorrow" marks his transition to the New Negro—a figure that is treated equally, one that is conscious of his beauty and confident that when his oppressors acknowledge it, they will be ashamed of the way they have treated him. That expectation, naïve though it may be, is part and parcel of his optimism.

No artist captured that optimism more memorably than the photographer James Van Der Zee, whose photographs document the invention of modern black identity. Many of the iconic images of the Harlem Renaissance—a couple wearing matching raccoon coats with the woman standing outside the Cadillac in which the man is seated, Marcus Garvey in full regalia in his roadster at a parade of the Universal Negro Improvement Association, the mass organization he led, the Abyssinian Baptist Church Sunday School—all are Van Der Zee photographs. He took his camera around Harlem, taking photos of social clubs and dinner parties, dancing schools and athletic teams. He composed portraits of the famous, including blues singer Mamie Smith, dancers Florence

Mills and Bill "Bojangles" Robinson, and the distinguished clergymen of Harlem. But they were not the source of his commercial success. His clients knew that he was adept at making those who were not at all famous look equally distinguished. In his words, "I could always see beauty where it didn't exist," and he would straighten out crossed eyes, close gaps between teeth, eliminate crows' feet and wrinkles, and sharpen noses to create the beauty that his clients could not see. Touched up and carefully lit, his photographs record people who know they are somebody, who are certain that their lives have meaning and value.

As much as Van Der Zee did to create images of New Negroes, as much as he staged portraits of them in their finery, he was keenly aware of the adversities that the camera concealed. In his studio, he kept a range of hand-painted backdrops, furniture, and props on hand so that his subjects could achieve the image of success they desired. He even had a selection of stylish clothing for those who had not acquired the means to dress up to their image of themselves. Couples came to celebrate engagements and weddings; they came back to have portraits made of their children. If a child died, his photograph might be taken in the casket, or, in the arms of his parents. When asked about the staging of one of the latter, Van Der Zee noted that the couple brought the dead child to the studio, where he arranged a home-like setting for the photograph. He explained that many children in Harlem died from pneumonia, because "it was a very common thing in those days for people to be without heat." That fact notwithstanding, his photographs focused on what his subjects *had*: a sense of optimism and possibility. If they have not achieved their goals, they remain confident that they could.

That optimistic spirit is endemic to Locke's conception of the New Negro as well. But unlike Hughes, whose poetic speakers are frequently female, Locke could only conceive of the New Negro as male. His imagery and his poetic allusions—to McKay, Hughes, and Cullen—are likewise male. Consequently he is silent on questions of gender and sexual identity, even though some of his peers raised those questions insistently.

The educator Elise Johnson McDougald was one of eight female contributors to *The New Negro*. Her article, "The Task of Negro Womanhood," was the only one to address the issue of gender. It is both a survey of black women's employment in the New York City labor force and a charge to successful black women to take up the cause of racial uplift. In contrast to Locke, McDougald concluded that the race was not free "economically, socially, or spiritually." In particular, she remarked on the challenges that the New Negro woman faced: "She is conscious that what is left of chivalry is not directed toward her. She realizes that the ideals of beauty, built up in the fine arts, have excluded her almost entirely. Instead the grotesque Aunt Jemimas of the street-car advertisements proclaim only an ability to serve without grace or loveliness." For Negro women, the day of "aunties," "uncles," and "mammies" was not gone; it still shadowed their attempt to forge new identities.

In "On Being Young—a Woman—and Colored," an essay published in 1925, Marita Bonner, a recent Radcliffe graduate, aspiring fiction writer and playwright, captured the complicated situation facing New Negro women in more personal terms. The stereotypes that Locke dismissed continued to haunt. Many of these were both sexist and racist: Bonner chafes at being perceived as "only a gross collection of desires." With her "sheepskin covered with sundry Latin phrases," she knows what she wants: a career, time ("the one real thing that money buys"), and "a husband you can look up to without looking down on yourself." But these desiderata are elusive. In the meantime, she feels torn between an obligation to less fortunate blacks, which leaves her "pinioned in the seaweed of a Black Ghetto" and life in the gilded ghetto of the black bourgeoisie with its endless cycle of movies, card games, and parties. She cannot complain about these options, privileged as she is: bitterness is not allowed. Addressing a female reader, presumably, as well educated and refined as she, who cannot plan even an excursion from Washington to New York without fear of offending propriety: "You decide that something is wrong with a world that stifles and chokes; that cuts off and stunts, hedging in, pressing down on eyes, ears and throat." Images of claustrophobia and stasis thread through the essay. It ends with a series of free associations, many of which reflect the persona's classical education. But after musing on the Greeks and Romans, the persona depicts herself as "still and quiet: motionless on the outside. But inside?" Though burdened by the demands of propriety, the need to be visibly virtuous, the persona retains a vital interior life. It is not one, however, that she can share.

Bonner's lyrical musings and the metaphors that convey them are echoed in the poetry and fiction of other women writers. In many of their poems, speakers travel through their imaginations, experiencing the mobility that Negro women were often denied in life. In a poem titled "Wishes," Georgia Douglas Johnson writes, "I'm tired of pacing the petty ring of the thing I/know— /I want to stand on the daylight's edge and see where the sunsets go." But after this opening, the poem transports the reader on a journey through a dreamscape. In contrast to the constraint and tedium of a life represented by "the petty round of the ring," the poem introduces images of physical and psychological freedom. Sailing through the limitless expanse of the sky, in flight as graceful as a bird, the speaker transcends time as well as space. From the point at which she stands "on the daylight's edge," she visualizes the night sky and her future. The desire to look seems as strong as the yearning to sail, which serves to underscore the extent of the speaker's current confinement. The poem does not specify the nature of that confinement; it seems plausible to infer that it is a version of the gilded ghetto Bonner describes. Defined or not, the forces that confine the speaker of "Wishes" will keep her earthbound. Her wishes will remain dreams deferred.

Some of the era's fictional protagonists also dream big. They want to expand their individual horizons as well as contribute to racial uplift. When those dreams are thwarted, the protagonists chafe against the constrictions of race and gender that thwart them. Most of them enjoy class privilege similar to that of their creators. But that privilege registers differently for them than for their black male and white female counterparts. When refracted through the prisms of racism and sexism, middle-class status is not the refuge that it first appears to be.

Angela Murray, the protagonist of Jessie Fauset's *Plum Bun* (1928), is a case in point. Her class status is achieved through her father, a caterer, and her mother, a one-time maid who now employs household help of her own. Angela and her sister Virginia are raised in a conservative Christian home; her father encourages them to be teachers. But Angela rejects the narrow path that her parents have prepared for her. She craves a wider range of experience and dreams of a career as an artist. Her mother has passed as a white woman all her life for convenience, to shop and eat at restaurants that are off-limits to Negroes. Without reckoning with the consequences, Angela also decides to pass in order to live the life she dreams about.

Passing was a popular subject for Harlem Renaissance writers, and the ability of some blacks to pass for white was a phenomenon that fascinated audiences. Articles on the topic appeared in mainstream newspapers. As Negroes were well aware, the NAACP official Walter White, who looked like a white man, slipped into southern towns to investigate lynchings. Of course, passing was not a new subject for American literature. Nineteenth-century authors including William Dean Howells and Harriet Beecher Stowe had exploited its dramatic and political potential. The pioneering African American novelist William Wells Brown had used it in *Clotel, or the President's Daughter*, published in England in 1853 because its fictionalization of the affair between Thomas Jefferson and Sally Hemings proved too incendiary to be published at home. In fact, Jefferson is not a character in the novel, which is devoted to the experiences of Clotel and her

The Harlem Renaissance

progeny. Clotel is visibly white yet tainted by her invisible black heritage and consequently destined to a life of despair that ends in an early death. She is the classic "tragic mulatto." Then in the twentieth century, black writers changed the script.

The fact that a character could register as black or white, depending on the circumstances, confirmed the fact that race, rather than something biologically determined, was a social construction. It was not a matter of complexion or hair texture, it was a matter of perception, and all the more arbitrary as a result. For some writers, like Fauset and James Weldon Johnson, the revelation of Negro identity was not a tragedy but an opportunity to lead a noble life. In *The Autobiography of an Ex-Colored Man*, Johnson represented race as a cultural identity, figured in the music that his protagonist played. In the strictly segregated society of the 1920s, white and blacks rarely interacted as equals. The Civic Club dinner was an exception, as noted in chapter 1, but it was a public event. Writers used mulatto characters as mediating figures to take readers inside white as well as black domestic spaces. They represented insider views of both.

In *Plum Bun* Angela moves from the black to the white world. Her ability to shift racial identities allows her to gauge the gains and losses each shift makes. As a colored woman, she lives constantly on edge, lest she be subjected to racial humiliation. She cannot imagine others in her race having the same high artistic ambitions that she has. Moreover, in even the most trivial pursuits, going to a movie or a restaurant for example, the possibility of racial humiliation looms. When the stakes are higher, for education or employment, the cost is computed in material as well as psychic terms. Her expulsion from art school in Philadelphia prompts her move to New York City, where she studies at Cooper Union and passes for white. As a white woman, Angela has access to educational and employment opportunities, comfortable housing—an apartment in Greenwich Village—and public accommodations. Her friends are white artists and intellectuals, who discuss politics and culture. Angela holds her own in their conversations. Most importantly, she moves freely through the world.

As a woman, however, she is subject to sexual exploitation by men. A cynical white acquaintance instructs Angela on the rule of modern courtship: "It is a game and the hardest game in the world for a woman, but the most fascinating.... [Y]ou have to be careful not to withhold too much and yet to give very little. If we don't give enough we lose them. If we give too much we lose ourselves." Bold in her naïvete, Angela looks forward to playing the game. She finds however that she cannot hold her own. She loses when, having run out of money, she submits to the white man who pursues her. Roger Fielding is a cad and a racist, yet Angela trades her self-respect for financial security. Her lowest point comes when she fails to acknowledge her sister Virginia in order to safeguard her affair.

She redeems herself when she declares her race to stand in solidarity with a black student, Rachel Powell, whose scholarship to study in France is rescinded when the funders discover her race. Angela's act enables the reconciliation with Virginia as owning the race is evidently tantamount to owning her sister. Still, Angela suffers consequences. She loses her job, and many of her progressive white friends deny her. She finds a refuge in Harlem before sailing for France. In the novel's most conservative turn, Angela makes marriage, not art, her goal. Retrospectively, she blames all of the "complications" in her life on her decision to pass.

No character in Nella Larsen's *Passing* (1929) makes such a judgment. Both of the main characters pass: Irene Redfield does so for reasons of convenience at a time when segregation was the rule even in northern cities, while Clare Kendry, married to a wealthy white racist, passes as a life choice. The novel opens in a Chicago hotel tearoom, where the two characters meet after years apart on an occasion when both are passing. Irene notices Clare staring at her and panics at the thought that her racial identity had been detected and she would be asked to leave. The scene highlights the ambiguity of racial identity. Negroes cannot always recognize other Negroes themselves, despite insisting that they can do so. Whites literally have no clue; race is not something that can be seen. For her part, Clare recognizes an old friend and feels nostalgic for the world she has left behind. Nostalgia spurs curiosity for that world, but Clare does not regret that she has left it.

Irene is a Harlem mother of two sons, whose physician husband's income provides a Harlem brownstone, car, and two servants. The price for security, even luxury, is a meaningless life. The character thinks of herself as a "race woman," but her work involves selling tickets to a fancy ball, a fund-raiser for the Negro Welfare League, a fictional organization based on the NAACP. Otherwise her life consists of the teas and bridge parties that Marita Bonner disdains in "On Being Young–A Woman–and Colored." Irene, on the other hand, is quite satisfied. Only her husband's dreams of trading his profession for a freer life in Brazil worry her. Clare disrupts the equilibrium that Irene works so hard to produce in her home. Clare visits uninvited and treats the servants too familiarly. She tries to chat with the children who largely ignore her. She fares better, much better, with the husband, who after warning Irene against renewing the friendship, is quickly captivated by Clare's insouciance.

Since the novel is narrated from Irene's point of view, readers see Clare only from her perspective. She is represented as alluring but dangerous, mysterious, and strange. Having "no allegiance beyond her own immediate desire, she was selfish, and cold, and hard. And yet she had, too, a strange capacity of transforming warmth and passion, verging sometimes almost on theatrical heroics." If Clare is dangerous, she is also warm and passionate. Whether drawn to the danger she represents or the warmth she recognizes, Irene cannot stay away. Passing enabled Clare to escape the poverty of her childhood. As she explains: "I was determined to get away, to be a person and not a charity or a problem, or even a daughter of the indiscreet Ham." She believes she has made the right deal. She has married a very wealthy man, an international banking agent; the couple has lived in various European capitals. In short, Clare has a life impossible for a colored woman in the 1920s.

For many colored women, middle class and otherwise, the need to be "respectable" was paramount. Any slip, even a too-tight dress or a too-loud laugh, could conjure up stereotypes of black women that dated back centuries. "A gross collection of desires," as Bonner put it. In *Passing*, Irene is ever on guard against conforming to any stereotype. She dresses stylishly, if conservatively; her home is flawlessly kept; and she is emotionally always under control. Clare, by contrast, is unconcerned with stereotypes. She dresses extravagantly, often lives in hotels, sends her daughter to boarding school, and frequently loses emotional control. Irene remembers Clare's "melodramatic grieving" when her father dies. She remembers the rumors that circulate about her as soon as Clare leaves home. On one occasion, Clare had been spotted with two white men and a white woman at a downtown hotel. The implication is clear: interracial encounters are assumed to be sexual.

They are certainly risky. In one scene Clare invites Irene and another childhood friend to her hotel suite. Her husband, Jack Bellew, arrives and greets Clare with the epithet "Nig." It does not occur to him that his wife's guests are not white. Called upon to explain himself, he remarks that Clare has gotten darker since they married, but she is not a Negro: "I draw the line at that. No niggers in my family. Never have been and never will be." Irene laughs, uncontrollably, but none of the women call Bellew on his racism. Irene rationalizes that she would not do so because of the risk to Clare. But given how angry she is at Clare for putting her in this situation, the rationalization is hard to credit. What is telling is that none of the women who are passing for white imagine that a white woman would protest racist comments.

Passing, like *Plum Bun*, is set in 1920s Harlem. The cultural awakening is the backdrop of both. A character based on Carl Van Vechten, the white novelist and bon vivant, shows up in Larsen's novel, while a character based on Du Bois shows up in Fauset's. With her focus on consciousness and interiority, however, Larsen writes a novel that is finally very different from *Plum Bun*. *Passing* is a modernist novel that does not represent the histories of its characters and only sketches the scenes that serve as the novel's backdrop. It moves quickly from the Harlem brownstone to the Chicago tearoom and hotel suite, then back to Harlem, to tea at the Redfields, the Negro Welfare Ball, and the walk-up apartment in which the last scene of the novel unfolds. The focus is on Irene's consciousness: her fears, insecurities, and unfulfilled desires. The novel is a complex, if ultimately unhappy portrait of a New Negro woman.

The lives of privileged women were represented in novels and paintings; their images were drawn on the covers of magazines. But the lives of working-class women gained less attention. There were a few exceptions. Anne Spencer's poem "Lady, Lady" is a lyrical tribute to an unnamed washerwoman: the title invests its subject with dignity. Certainly, the poem is a departure for Spencer, who was primarily a meditative poet. Although she was a civil rights activist in Lynchburg, Virginia, Spencer steered clear of social and political issues in her writing. This poem's subject is described "as dark as night." The physical effects of her labor are visible in her wrinkled, bleached-white hands. In these descriptions the poem protests the exploitation of the woman's labor, but it also draws a vivid contrast between her hands and her heart. In a direct address to the subject, the poem's final quatrain declares, "Lady, Lady, I saw your heart, / And altered there in its darksome place, / Were the tongues of flame the ancients knew, / Where the good God sits to spangle through." More than nobility, the poem attributes the gift of poetry to the "Lady." The subject does not, however, speak for herself. Spencer's language and allusions serve to hold the subject at a distance.

Readers encounter close up the maids and laundresses who people Zora Neale Hurston's fiction and Langston Hughes's poetry and fiction. The language of their texts evokes the speech spoken by working-class black women. In the short story "Sweat," for example, Hurston's protagonist Delia Jones washes others people's clothes for a living. Her language infuses vernacular speech with biblical idiom. In Hughes's novel, *Not Without Laughter*, the protagonist's grandmother is an "old Negro" in every respect, including her willingness to serve whites; she is nonetheless an inspiration to her grandson. One of her daughters is a snob who reads *The Crisis*. Another is a blues singer, who having learned the traditional blues from her brother-in-law, is by the end of the novel performing at the Lafayette, one of Harlem's leading vaudeville houses.

The classic blues singers, on whom Hughes based his character, told the stories of ordinary black women that writers generally did not tell. Ida Cox, Ma Rainey, Bessie Smith, Clara Smith, and Mamie Smith, who were not related to each other, came to fame in the 1920s. With their fur boas and fancy gowns, jewelry and expensive cars, they lived lives their fans could only dream of. Yet the songs they sang reflected the loves and losses, the hard times, and endless labor that their listeners recognized as their own. The blues women did not concern themselves with the politics of respectability, but they were keenly aware of the pain of being called out of one's name. In "Young Woman's Blues," Bessie Smith sang:

> Some people call me a hobo, some call me a bum
> Nobody knows my name, nobody knows what I've done
> I'm as good as any woman in your town
> I ain't high yeller, I'm a deep killa brown
> I'm ain't gonna marry, ain't gonna settle down
> I'm gonna drink good moonshine and run these browns down.

Smith's persona refuses to accept the judgment of the respectable women in her town. She knows who she is (fig. 3). She knows she

3. Bessie Smith's fans dubbed her the "Empress of the Blues," both for her incomparable artistry and her glamorous image.

is as good as anyone else, despite her dark skin and unconventional behavior; she drinks and she has sex with the partners she chooses. Marriage is not a goal: pleasure is. The first stanza of the song refers to chickens crowing, and the reference to moonshine further identifies the speaker as rural and southern. She claims her own identity, and it has nothing to do with the

Harlem intelligentsia. The bravado of the lyrics is echoed in the pulsing rhythm of the musical accompaniment.

In the end though, the song is a blues…and the persona's determination is hard won:

> See that long lonesome road
> Lord, you know it's gotta end
> I'm a good woman and I can get plenty men.

The boast is not an empty one but neither is it triumphant. However many lovers she can attract, the road ahead is long and lonesome. Only the Lord knows when it will end. In the meantime, she will rely on her own compass and make the journey by herself.

Blues lyrics gave voice to feelings that would otherwise have had no public expression. Sexual relationships were a frequent topic, but the blues had none of the romance of Tin Pan Alley. There was no moonlight, love did not last, partners cheated, and right did not trump wrong. Sexuality was adult and complex; it did not fit neatly into socially acceptable categories. In their private lives, Ma Rainey and Bessie Smith were bisexuals. Rainey's song, "Prove It On Me," recorded in 1928, made the private public. Ma Rainey's persona dared any one to prove that she had a sexual relationship with a woman. It was true, the lyrics allowed, that the friends she had been with the night before "must've been women, 'cause I don't like no men." She acknowledged that she wears a collar and a tie; still, she is not putting any more of her business in the street: "They say I do it, ain't nobody caught me, / They sure got to prove it on me." Even the denial is a confirmation. Blues women were "out" in a way that their literary peers were not.

Countee Cullen, Langston Hughes, Alain Locke, and Claude McKay kept their homosexuality private. In the last three decades scholars have "outed" them, based on biographical evidence drawn mainly from the authors' correspondence and interviews with people who knew them, and textual evidence, drawn from inferences and allusions in their writing. Much of the evidence is persuasive, which makes the writers' silences on sexual identity all the more poignant. In the 1920s homosexuality was illegal. As black men who were also artists, these writers might have concluded that they were outsiders enough. One writer who was black and out was Richard Bruce Nugent, who not only lived the life but wrote about it.

"Smoke, Lilies and Jade" was Nugent's contribution to *Fire!!*, where it appeared alongside Hughes's and Cullen's poetry and Hurston's "Sweat." Nugent's prose poem looks like none of them. The piece is a stream-of-consciousness interior monologue written in sentence fragments punctuated by ellipses. Past events fuse with those in the present in Alex, the protagonist's mind. The form suits the content, a jumble of unconscious thoughts and feelings around the death of Alex's father years before. At that time, his mother had ordered him not to cry and to be a man. Now nineteen, jobless, and living a decadent life in New York, he continues to fail the test of manhood as his mother and society define it.

Oscar Wilde is his model. Alex thinks of himself as a writer, but he writes nothing. He smokes constantly, drinks excessively, and parties with a host of literary luminaries, including Hughes, Hurston, and Toomer. Falling short of their standard, Alex congratulates himself on making their acquaintance. But the incessant name-dropping only highlights his failures. Yet, the writing makes clear that Alex *is* an artist; he manipulates words and images to create a memorable portrait of himself. In some moments he employs synesthesia, the use of colors to represent feelings, to add texture to his portrait and avers, "oh the joy of being an artist and of blowing blue smoke thru an ivory holder inlaid with red jade and green." Beyond the literary techniques he hones, his joy in his vocation is the best evidence of his status as artist. His descriptions of his two lovers speak to his sexual identity. The young man he calls Beauty and the woman named Melva are both "perfect" and complementary. The scenes recounting the lovemaking between Alex and Beauty are initially set in a dreamscape of blue smoke, black poppies, and red calla lilies; then Alex wakes up in the bed they share.

Its editor Wallace Thurman subtitled *Fire!!* "A Quarterly Devoted to the Younger Negro Artists" and hoped it would scandalize their elders. Doubtless, some leaders found the topics of the journal unseemly, and none could have offended them more than Nugent's writing. His devotion to the pursuit of pleasure rendered him an unlikely participant in the New Negro movement; his work could obviously not advance a political struggle. Yet Nugent's writings and drawings compelled his audience to consider sexuality as a component in identity. Fewer than a handful of artists—including the novelist Wallace Thurman, the poet Mae Cowdery and the sculptor Richmond Barthé—dared represent its importance. But as New Negroes redefined themselves, they also faced the fact that identity was more than a matter of race. It involved interlocking factors of gender, class, sexuality, and psychology that could not be untangled.

The most eloquent statement for the right of artists to write about what they chose came from Langston Hughes in his 1926 essay "The Negro Artist and the Racial Mountain." Speaking for himself, for writers, and for artists in various genres, Hughes acknowledged the pressure on artists from whites who wanted their stereotypes of blacks confirmed and from Negroes who wanted ennobling images. To do anything worthwhile, he averred, artists had to be true to themselves. Poor blacks provided an example of the autonomy Hughes called on artists to cultivate. They ignored the calls for respectability made by middle-class blacks; they did not try to conform to white standards. They also left artists alone. Bourgeois blacks, by contrast, were all too quick to criticize Negro artists, although slow to support their work.

Hughes doubted their ability to understand his art, deaf as he claimed they were to the beauty of the spirituals, blues, and jazz that inspired it. In the face of criticism and neglect, Hughes declared the artistic independence of a generation:

> We younger Negro artists who create now intend to express our dark-skinned selves without fear or shame. If white people are pleased we are glad. If they are not, it doesn't matter. We know we are beautiful. And ugly too. The tom-tom cries and the tom-tom laughs. If colored people are pleased we are glad. If they are not, their displeasure doesn't matter either. We build our temples for tomorrow, strong as we know how, and stand on top of the mountain, free within ourselves.

Chapter 3
Harlem: City of dreams

This is not water running here,
These thick rebellious streams
That hurtle flesh and bone past fear
Down alleyways of dreams.

This is a wine that must flow on
Not caring how or where,
So it has ways to flow upon
Where song is in the air.

So it can woo an artful flute
With loose, elastic lips,
In measurement of joy compute
With blithe, ecstatic hips.

Countee Cullen, "Harlem Wine" (1925)

Harlem was the dream capital of black America. In letters home, recent arrivals boasted of the great housing, good jobs, schools, and churches. Hundreds of thousands answered the call. Most found the fancy apartment buildings beyond their means, but even substandard housing in Harlem was better than the tin-roofed cabins of the rural South. Most of the jobs available to blacks in New York were menial, but they paid much better than the agricultural wages common in the South. If few migrants could afford to frequent the clubs that gave Harlem its glamorous veneer, they could hear great music at local bars and house parties. Their children could attend public schools. They could choose from an array of churches with worship styles as austere or demonstrative as they wished. If they ran out of money, they could entertain themselves by strolling along the broad promenade of Seventh Avenue. Free of the surveillance of the Ku Klux Klan and the white terror that threatened black life in the South, they could embrace a sense of freedom. "I'd rather be a lamp post in Harlem than governor of Georgia" went one popular saying. For many, there was no place they would rather be.

Beyond the material realities, there was something special about Harlem that could not be pinned down. Countee Cullen tried to capture it in his poem "Harlem Wine." The life force of Harlem, as elemental as water, is transfigured here as wine. It symbolizes the spirit of the people who come there to pursue their dreams but find that those dreams are up against harsh realities. The newcomers are not dissuaded: the wine "must flow on," and a rebellious spirit is necessary to stay the course. That spirit expresses itself through music ("the artful flute") and dance. Consequently, the dance is an expression both of rebellion and of joy too profound to measure. The poem speaks both to the jazz that brought pleasure to ordinary Harlemites and to the music that was the poet's muse.

If, for black workers emigrating from the South or the Caribbean, Harlem was the city of dreams, intellectuals deemed it the Culture Capital, the greatest Negro city in the world, the mecca of the New Negro, and the City of Refuge. Harlem was the physical embodiment of the spirit of the New Negro, and it was indisputably modern. The largest black community in the United States, located as it was in the national cultural capital, Harlem logically became the main setting of the renaissance. But logic was not all there was to it. James Weldon Johnson, one of its earliest historians, offers an evocative description:

Harlem is indeed the great Mecca for the sight-seer, the pleasure-seeker, the curious, the adventurous, the enterprising, the ambitious and the talented of the whole Negro world; for the lure of it has reached down to every island of the Carib Sea and has penetrated even into Africa.

Johnson's Harlem was cosmopolitan. Most of its residents had migrated from the rural South and others were native New Yorkers, a significant number came from the Caribbean (representing perhaps 20 percent of the population), and a small number from Africa. The demographic mix produced myriad opportunities for exchange as well as conflict, as people became aware of a black world much wider than they had imagined. Johnson, himself a cosmopolite, who had achieved success in education, the law, the theater, and the diplomatic service, knew firsthand how broadly diverse black cultures were. As blacks from different backgrounds interacted in Harlem, they recognized the breadth of experiences as well. Although Johnson, an ardent integrationist, would not have credited it, *Negro World*, the weekly newspaper of Garvey's Universal Negro Improvement Association (UNIA), contributed to this knowledge by reporting international news and featuring a column that was published in rotation in French, Spanish, and Portuguese, the European languages spoken across the African diaspora.

As a mecca for the curious and the adventurous, Harlem drew pleasure seekers. Although it would take until 1937 for Rodgers and Hart to pen the tune "The Lady is a Tramp," in which the lady "won't go to Harlem in ermine and pearls," Harlem had a reputation in the 1920s as a place for rich whites to go "slumming." Certain clubs—including the Cotton Club (fig. 4), Connie's Inn, and the black-owned Barrons—catered to this clientele. Black Harlem had its own favorites: Tillie's Chicken Shack, Pud's and Jerry's, and Mexico's, all conveniently located on the same block as the Clam House, where Gladys Bentley performed, on West 133rd Street between Lenox and Seventh.

4. Although Maude Russell's claim to have invented the Charleston was false, she and her troupe, the Ebony Steppers, showcased the dance in nightclubs such as the Cotton Club, shown here in 1929.

Carl Van Vechten, a popular novelist and well-known pleasure seeker, became notorious for leading white writers and celebrities on after-hours tours of Harlem. William Faulkner and his publisher Bennett Cerf were two of those who went "inspectin' with Van Vechten," as the songwriter Andy Razaf put it. Van Vechten knew the hot spots, including those that served a Negro clientele. Although he was something of a voyeur, he was also a serious student of the blues, and friend and patron to black writers such as Langston Hughes and Nella Larsen. Moreover, Van Vechten and his wife, the actress Fania Marinoff, hosted interracial parties at their West 55th Street apartment, where George Gershwin and Tallulah Bankhead might share drinks with Paul Robeson and Walter White, the convivial field secretary of the NAACP. Bessie Smith and her entourage attended a party that has entered into legend. Smith refused the martinis that her host served and asked for her gin straight. She listened to an aria, sung by Marguerite d'Alvarez whom she complimented: "Don't let *nobody* tell you *you* can't sing." But when Marinoff tried to kiss her good-bye, Smith threw a punch and screamed, "Get the fuck away from me. I ain't never heard of such shit." Of course she had kissed and been kissed by women, but she reserved the prerogative to choose whom and when.

In a move that irritated many of the Harlemites who had welcomed him uptown, in 1926 Van Vechten published a novel titled *Nigger Heaven*. It became the best-selling novel of the Harlem Renaissance. (Claude McKay's *Home to Harlem* was runner-up.) Some Negroes could not forgive the title or the content. The main plot told the story of New Negro professionals who struggled to hold on to their hopes even as their ambitions were continuously thwarted by racism. The more memorable subplot was fueled by cocaine, orgies, and Satan worship. Both plots were exaggerated. Mary Love, the protagonist was both high-minded and insipid. Lasca Sartoris, the evil seductress, also strains the reader's credulity. This is not to say that cocaine-sniffing seductresses were not part of the Harlem landscape, but devil-worshippers were too few to count.

Harlem did boast its own adventurer in Hubert Fauntleroy Julian, a handsome Trinidadian-born pilot, whom the New York press dubbed the "Black Eagle." After serving in the Royal Canadian Air Corps during the war, Julian moved to Harlem, where he became an officer in Marcus Garvey's UNIA. Dressed in full aviator gear, he twice parachuted into Harlem, in 1922 and 1923; the second time he played a gold-plated saxophone as he descended. Both times he missed the announced target, but he did not disappoint his fans. Figures like Julian were imaginable only in Harlem; they could only reimagine themselves there.

The same might be said of Alexander Gumby, a bellhop by day and bon vivant by night. Richard Bruce Nugent, himself a Harlem dandy, penned this portrait of Gumby: "Fancy clothes, a perennial walking stick, pale yellow kid gloves and a diamond stick-pin helped make him the Beau Brummel of his particular little group." In that group he was known as "The Count." He established "Gumby's Bookstore" in his apartment on Fifth Avenue off 125th Street to house his extensive collection of rare books and *objêts d'art*. Between 1926 and 1930, the apartment was a popular gathering place for New Negro writers and artists. Writers signed books, painters displayed their work, and musicians held recitals in the space, where copious food and drink were always on tap. Gumby's own artistic expression took the form of handmade scrapbooks—more than 140 in all—that document his idiosyncratic perspective on Negro history and culture.

Most Harlemites reinvented themselves on a more modest scale. Weldon Johnson trumpeted the achievements of the enterprising and the talented in his essay "Harlem: The Culture Capital," which was published in *The New Negro*. The essay documented the history of blacks in New York (he would later write a book on the subject, titled *Black Manhattan*). Both charted the upward movement of blacks from Greenwich Village to the Tenderloin district, where most lived at the turn of the twentieth century, to Harlem. In fact, Harlem was not even a part of Manhattan until 1873. Named after the Dutch village of Haarlem, the area had been a farming village throughout most of the eighteenth and nineteenth centuries. After the agricultural value of the land was depleted, it became a favorite spot for Sunday excursions in the country. In the 1870s, Harlem was transformed into an upper and upper-middle-class suburb—Manhattan's first. The townhouses in Striver's Row (138th and 139th Streets between Seventh and Eighth Avenues, now Adam Clayton Powell and Frederick Douglass Boulevard) were built in the 1890s and designed by prominent architects, including Stanford White, whose structures include the arch at Washington Square and the second Madison Square Garden. The spacious ten- to twelve-room brownstones, set back from the street for greater privacy, equipped with rear entrances for servants, included alleys in which horse-drawn carriages could be parked. Yet, upon completion, some of the houses on Striver's Row, an epithet bestowed by black Harlemites in the 1920s, could not find buyers.

Ironically, blacks, some newly arrived from the South, were the first to rent in several of Harlem's most elegant buildings. This came about largely through the business acumen of the realtor Philip A. Payton, a Republican politico Charles Anderson, and the businessman John Nail, the father-in-law of James Weldon Johnson. These entrepreneurs were not alone: St. Philip's Episcopal Church paid more than a million dollars for a row of buildings on 135th Street, between Lenox and Seventh Avenues, just around the corner from its new edifice on 134th Street. The church, originally founded in 1809 in lower Manhattan, was one of the first congregations to relocate to Harlem, as the locus of black New York moved northward. Between 1911 and 1922, most of the large black churches—St. James Presbyterian, Mother A. M. E. Zion, and Abyssinian Baptist—moved to Harlem. According to Adam Clayton Powell Sr., the Abyssinian pastor and father of the future congressman, Harlem "became the symbol of liberty and the Promised Land to Negroes everywhere."

Black professionals followed their clients uptown. Accountants and attorneys hung out their shingles, and Harlem Hospital became the first hospital in New York City to grant privileges to Negro physicians. Entrepreneurs seized opportunity and opened grocery stores, meat markets, drug stores, funeral homes, beauty parlors, barbershops, and florists. In 1928 Dunbar National Bank opened in the cooperative apartment complex sponsored by the Rockefellers and named in honor of the poet Paul Laurence Dunbar (fig. 5). It was a reminder that not every business was the measure of racial progress it seemed to be, as some establishments turned out to be black-managed rather than black-owned. Social clubs and fraternal organizations—the Prince Hall Masons, the Benevolent and Protective Order of Elks—and their female auxiliaries established headquarters in Harlem. Negro newspapers

(*New York Age* and *Amsterdam News*) soon arrived to chronicle the goings-on.

One entrepreneur stood out above the rest. Madame C. J. Walker, born Sarah Breedlove in Louisiana in the 1860s, was the first African American female millionaire. The source of her fortune was a hair-straightening process, or as she preferred to call it, a hair-growing process, which had come to her in a dream. The circumstances differed, depending on the account, but the bottom line was the same: a widowed washerwoman, who was desperate to support her only child, Walker magically came into possession of a secret formula—some ingredients were said to come all the way from Africa—that transformed nappy hair into silken locks. By the time she arrived in New York in 1914, she was a woman of means. She had established a manufacturing plant in Indianapolis

5. The staff of Dunbar National Bank embodied the confidence and ambition of Harlem's New Negroes. Established in 1928, the bank held on during the early years of the Depression but folded after a decade.

and a chain of salons across the United States and in parts of
Central America and the West Indies. These salons were the
exclusive distributors of her products. In the center of Harlem—in
two brownstones on 136th Street between Lenox and Seventh
Avenues—she set up headquarters and founded the Walker
College of Hair Culture. She designated her daughter, A'Lelia
Walker Robinson, as manager and installed her in one of the
buildings' well-appointed apartments. Madame Walker devoted
her time to plans for her suburban estate, located in Irvington-on-
Hudson and named Villa Lewaro, thanks to Enrico Caruso's
acronym in honor of A'*Le*lia *Wa*lker *Ro*binson. Designed by the
African American architect V. W. Tandy, the Italianate mansion
boasted thirty-four rooms, including a library, conservatory,
billiard room, and gymnasium; a drawing room that measured
21 x 32 feet was just off the marble foyer. Completed in 1917, the
house was built for entertaining. Members of Harlem's elite, who
would have had nothing to do with the Sarah Breedlove from
Louisiana, craved invitations to Madame's soirees. In the
meantime, back in Harlem, A'Lelia, whom Langston Hughes
deemed "the joy goddess of Harlem," hosted legendary parties at
the salon she named "The Dark Tower," after the poem by Countee
Cullen. A businesswoman after a fashion, A'Leilia charged for the
refreshments served at her parties. Many of the young writers, for
whom (they thought) the salon had been established, could often
not afford the prices.

The development of Harlem as the "mecca of the New Negro"
coincided with the arrival of tens of thousands of southern blacks
in the city. Trading their familiar if oppressive lives in Virginia,
North Carolina, South Carolina, and Georgia for the promised
opportunity of the North, they arrived daily at the Pennsylvania
Railroad Station. Many took the subway up to Harlem; their
arrivals expanded the neighborhood's borders and by the end of
the 1920s, Harlem stretched from the northern edge of Central
Park at 110th Street to 155th Street and west from Lenox to St.
Nicholas Avenue. The area was now more than 70 percent black.

As many newcomers struggled to pay the rent, some took in boarders and others hosted rent parties, which were the most inventive response to a necessity. Featuring great music, often recorded but sometimes performed live by Harlem's famous stride pianists James P. Johnson, Willie "the Lion" Smith, and Thomas "Fats" Waller, and serving downhome dishes, the parties were so popular that sometimes they were held even when no rent was due.

If Harlem as a city-within-a-city conveyed a nationalistic spirit, it also represented the fulfillment of an assimilationist dream. Anyone walking or riding through the community could see how much like the rest of New York City it was. With broad avenues, spacious apartment buildings, and handsome brownstones, Harlem could have been an extension of the Upper West Side— except for the race of its residents. Johnson believed that its location guaranteed that Harlem would never become a ghetto.

For Johnson, whose ideas owed something to the philosophy of Booker T. Washington, property ownership was a measure of progress. He tells the story of a woman who sold pig feet and fried chicken at the corner of 135th Street and Lenox Avenue and was known to her customers as "Pig Foot Mary." Johnson reveals her identity to be Mrs. Mary Dean, the owner of a five-story apartment building before she sold it to the Y.W.C.A. to be used as a dormitory. Even someone who looked the part of the Old Negro, Johnson seemed to argue, had the enterprising as well as the civic spirit of a New Negro. Pig Foot Mary deserved respect, as the title "Mrs." conferred. Of course, Mrs. Dean was hardly typical; most Harlemites were renters, but her story speaks to the possibilities for self-invention that Harlem symbolized.

Harlem's promise lured writers as well as ordinary folk. In Langston Hughes's words, it "was like a great magnet for the Negro intellectual, pulling him from everywhere." Aspiring writers flocked to the community: In 1925 Rudolph Fisher, a newly minted physician, came from Washington to pursue careers in both literature and medicine. After his two-year fellowship at Columbia University's College of Physicians and Surgeons, he set up practice as an X-ray specialist. His keen-eyed observations of Harlem by day and by night would be the focus of his essays, short stories, and novels. Arna Bontemps, a Louisiana native, and the Utah-born Wallace Thurman came to Harlem from California, where they were both employed at the Los Angeles post office. Knowing that both were aspiring writers, their co-workers introduced them to each other. When Bontemps's first poem was published by the *Crisis* in 1924, he recollected that he "(a) received a copy of the August issue, which carried my poem, (b) resigned my job in the post office, and (c) packed my suitcase and bought a ticket to New York City." He later remembered Harlem of the 1920s as "a foretaste of paradise." Thurman arrived a year later. His 1928 play *Harlem*, co-authored with William Jourdan Rapp, dramatized the conflicts around race, class, and ethnicity that the newcomers encountered. Like most migrants, Zora Neale Hurston moved north in stages, starting from her home in Eatonville, Florida, to Memphis, Baltimore, and Washington, D.C. She arrived in New York in January 1925 with "$1.50, no job, no friends and a lot of hope." Born in British Guiana (now Guyana), Eric Waldrond had arrived in 1918, from Panama, where his Barbadian-born father, like many other West Indians of his generation, found work building the canal. Waldrond at nineteen believed *his* dreams could be realized in New York. By 1925 he was the business manager of *Opportunity* and a well-published author.

In Harlem the young writers met members of the Old Guard leadership, which included W. E. B. Du Bois and James Weldon Johnson, both of whom lived in the exclusive section of Harlem known as Sugar Hill. Du Bois had lived in New York since founding the *Crisis* in 1910. Historian and sociologist, philosopher anonymity, the shredding of old values, and the disintegration of families.

In his story "The City of Refuge," Rudolph Fisher captures the way that Harlem could dazzle the imaginations of newcomers as well as the complex realities that they sometimes failed to negotiate. The ironically named King Solomon Gillis, on the lam after killing a white man in self-defense in North Carolina, is disoriented by the clamor of Penn Station when he arrives in New York. The subway ride uptown further jangles his nerves. But when he climbs the steps at the 135th Street station, he feels that he has entered a haven that, despite all that he has heard about it, he could not fully imagine beforehand. Harlem is a place where "black is white," that is, where blacks are in control. Gillis responds to it with a mixture of insight ("you had rights that could not be denied you, you had privileges, protected by law") and naïveté ("And you had money. Everybody in Harlem had money"). The sight of a black policeman (fig. 6) is confirmation that he has reached the promised land: "Done died an' woke up in Heaven," he exclaims, then repeats like an incantation, "even got cullud policemens."

Gazing on the unimaginable scene, Gillis does not realize that Mouse Uggam, a con man, is sizing him up. Mouse plays on the fact that he and Gillis are from the same town, a coincidence that strain[s] redulity. But the textured representation of Harlem is completely [c]onvincing. As Gillis first takes in the Harlem streetscape, he is [st]ruck by the plenitude of blackness: "Negroes predominantly, [o]verwhelming everywhere. There was assuredly no doubt of his [w]hereabouts. This was Negro Harlem." Later he recognizes the [di]fferences that the visible blackness obscures. Some of the people [in] the street speak an urban vernacular that Gillis needs to decod[e;] [d]ines" are working-class blacks and "jay birds" are new arrivals l[ike] [him]self. Initially, he is appalled by the intraracial prejudice that [bla]cks born in the United States show toward blacks from the [Car]ibbean, but he soon uses the epithet "monkey-chaser" himself

and poet, Du Bois was by any accounting the foremost intellectual of the race; had the nation not been so riven by racial discrimination, he would have been counted as the leading American intellectual that he was. He might have had the Ivy League professorship commensurate with his academic attainments; instead he was an independent scholar, journal editor, and "race man." He had doubts about the young writers, mostly because they seemed more interested in artistic expression than in the struggle for race progress. James Weldon Johnson had a broader perspective. A man of the theater, he had written revues with his brother J. Rosamund and William Cole; their song, "Under the Bamboo Tree," was a hit. A true renaissance man, Weldon Johnson had also been a school principal, a lawyer, a poet, and a diplomat. In 1912 he published the novel *The Autobiography of an Ex-Colored Man*, but he did so anonymously. When it was reissued in 1927, Johnson signed his name. The novel is a fictional coming-of-age story of a mulatto or biracial man in the post-Reconstruction era. Unlike the unnamed protagonist who passes for white and recognizes, too late, that he has sold his birthright for a mess of pottage, Johnson was a dedicated race man and a citizen of the arts.

Jessie Fauset moved to New York when she became the literary editor of the *Crisis* in 1919. Working for Du Bois, whose hauteur was as legendary as his brilliance, she frequently sought out and was sought out by young writers whom Du Bois had intimidated. Fauset wrote Arna Bontemps the letter that changed his life by prompting his move to Harlem. When she wrote Jean Toomer in February 1922 to accept two of his poems, she offered her continued support: "I cannot tell you how vividly your work has renewed my interest in you. When I see you I feel as though I should like to assist you in putting the world at [your?] feet." Upon receiving Langston Hughes's poem, "The Negro Speaks of Rivers," Fauset recalled five years later in the March 1926 *Crisis*, she took "the beautiful dignified creation" to Dr. Du Bois and said: "What colored person is there, do you suppose, in the United States who writes like that and yet is unknown to us?" She was determined to seek him out; when Hughes started his year at Columbia, she invited him to the Civic Club to lunch with her and Du Bois.

Fauset loved the theater. Among the first things she did when she moved to New York was to volunteer as an usher at *Shuffle Along*. Claude McKay, who disdained middle-class blacks in his writing and in person, noted that despite being "prim, pretty, and well dressed," Fauset was liked by all the radicals, "although in her social viewpoint she was away over on the other side of the fence." Whatever their politics and whether they found her to be charming and a good conversationalist, writers understood that Fauset had the power to publish their work. Most were happy to please her, but even when they disappointed her, as Hughes did when he wrote about the underside of Harlem and rejected traditional lyric poetry for poetry inflected by jazz and blues, she did not withdraw her support.

Hughes, who would eventually be considered the "Poet Laureate of Harlem," found the greatest Negro city in the world a source of endless inspiration. He set poems in cabarets, storefront churches, and railroad flats. Keenly attuned to Harlem's sounds, he wrote blues and jazz poems as well as poems inspired by gospel shouts. Harlem was a gift to all the writers who lived there, and they set numerous poems, short stories, and novels against its backdrop. Writers limned the streetscape of Harlem, echoed its soundscape, and celebrated its spirit. They depicted its people in their rich variety, in terms as superficial as complexion and as serious as class. The kaleidoscope of complexions within the race became a literary trope, as this representative passage from Rudolph Fisher's novel, *The Walls of Jericho* (1928) shows:

> Consider the mere item of complexion, you whose choice may only run from cool white to warm rose-and-olive. Harlem offers its cool white too, with blue eyes and flaxen hair, believe it or not; proceeds

on through the conventional shades to the warmth of rose-and-olive; and here, where the rest of Manhattan ends, Harlem has just begun: through the creams, the honeys, and high-browns, the browns, the sealskins and chestnuts—a dozen gradations in every class, not one without its peculiar richness.

If, as Fisher avows, one could find a richer variety of beauty in black Harlem than in white Manhattan, he was aware that complexion was often a marker of class among black America. In his fiction he depicted conflicts between middle-class, light skinned blacks and their darker-skinned working-class neighl In the end, with the deft comic touch that was his trademark, represents them making common cause.

Writers like Fisher could not resist the language of Harlem. Southern idioms meshed with urban slang to produce a fresh vernacular. In "A Glossary of Harlem Slang," Zora Neale Hurst listed some definitions: "balling" meant having fun, "gut-bucke referred to a low-down dive as well as the music that was playe there, "ofay" referred to a white person, and "dicty" referred to high-toned black. Several novels included glossaries so that re could keep up with the fast-changing vocabulary, and many w tried with varying success to transcribe and stylize the speecl heard on the street. Although some of the efforts are cringe- a few writers succeeded in rendering the oral literate.

In addition to the language, writers explored the folkways Harlem—the Sunday promenades, the religious services, ₐ ubiquitous rent parties. They described local culinary delⁱ with care. Several described the game of numbers, a gam game often called "Harlem's favorite indoor sport." Some the harsher realities: the hard work and racial discrimin were the lot of many Harlemites. More than the race leₐ boosters, writers were eager to probe behind the façad₆ measure the cost of the northern migration. They wouˈ the alienation that some southerners experienced in F

6. Police officer Rubin Cortes directs traffic on the corner of Harlem's West 135th Street and Lenox Avenue around 1925. Rudolph Fisher's short story "City of Refuge" captures the stunned response of newly arrived southern migrants to the existence of black policemen.

Whites are not simply whites either. Mouse manipulates Gillis into a job with an Italian grocer, who speaks his own vernacular and proves as gullible about the underside of Harlem life as Gillis. The strict binary between black and white that governed Gillis's life in the South is unsettled. Gillis realizes too late that in the North, it is often the black people that he cannot trust.

"The City of Refuge" tells a story that became part of Harlem lore. The gullible southerner ends up caught in a drug ring—here the drug is "French medicine"—and takes the fall. Fifty years after Fisher published his story, Stevie Wonder would tell an updated version in his song, "Living for the City," that includes a voice-over in which a judge sentences the man to ten years. The man responds, "What?" Gillis cannot believe what has happened to him either, but his disbelief has as much to do with the very idea of Harlem as with his particular situation. Even as he is arrested, he repeats the mantra "even-got-cullud-policemens" with a new insistence: "and the grin that came over his features had something exultant about it." Gillis's delusions negate the possibility for self-invention.

Among the period's most poignant expressions of dislocation is Claude McKay's poem "The Tropics in New York." It depicts the reaction of its speaker to a store window filled with fruits that remind him of home. The fact that they are sealed behind glass highlights the paradox in the poem's title:

> Bananas ripe and green, and ginger-root,
> Cocoa in pods and alligator pears,
> And tangerine and mangoes and grape fruit,
> Fit for the highest prize at parish fairs.
>
> Set in the window, bringing memories
> Of fruit-trees laden by low-singing rills,
> And dewy-dawn, and mystical blue skies
> In benediction over nun-like hills.
>
> My eyes grew dim, and I could no more gaze;
> A wave of longing through my body swept,
> And hungry for the old, familiar ways,
> I turned aside and bowed my head and wept.

Capturing the fusion of pleasure and pain that defines nostalgia, the poem begins with a sonorous catalog of tropical fruits and ends with the speaker in tears. Several of the fruits are not native to the United States, and the metric pattern of their naming renders them both delicious and strange. The second stanza draws the contrast between fruit that is sold in stores and the fruit growing in nature. Words with spiritual connotations ("mystical," "benediction," "nun-like") make the memories seem precious and the realities they invoke more distant. The words also anticipate the impact that his reveries have on the speaker. Brought to tears by the power of his memories, the speaker accepts the fact that he is unlikely to go home anytime soon. But the poem redefines what is familiar and what is strange. The exotic fruits and the uncommon references ("parish fairs," "rills") are rendered familiar while the way of life in New York becomes strange. Compelled to identify with the speaker, the reader can empathize with his loss.

Despite his broad travels, Harlem had a hold on Claude McKay. In his memoir, *A Long Way From Home,* he wrote of one return: "A wave of thrills flooded the arteries of my being, and I felt as if I had undergone initiation as a member of my tribe. And I was happy. Yes, it was a rare sensation again to be just one black among many. It was good to be lost in the shadows of Harlem again." The promise of belonging is indeed thrilling, as the physiological changes it elicits confirm. Yet Harlem also offers a guarantee of anonymity, of being "lost in the shadows of Harlem." That anonymity offers a measure of psychological freedom that is not available when one is black in a white world, even for a cosmopolite like McKay.

Harlem was certainly an inspiration for McKay as a writer. After winning fame in the United States for "If We Must Die," he expanded and retitled a volume of poems first published in England as *Springtime in New Hampshire* (McKay had worked at a resort hotel in the Granite State); it became *Harlem Shadows* when it was published in the United States in 1922. Several of the poems are set in Harlem. "Harlem Dancer," along with the title poem, uses the fallen-woman trope in ways that are as conventional as the poem's diction and Shakespearean meter. In 1928 McKay published *Home to Harlem* and in 1940 *Harlem: Negro Metropolis,* an idiosyncratic collection of essays that includes chapters on cults and occultists, and the numbers game, along with essays on businessmen and politicians.

Home to Harlem has a feather of a plot. When the novel opens, the protagonist Jake is working on a European freighter while taking a circuitous journey home after the Great War. Jake has enlisted in the war, although the novel represents this as an impulsive decision. Black and brawny, Jake acts intuitively, not reflectively. On his first night back in Harlem, he hooks up with a prostitute, loses her, and spends the rest of the novel in search of her. Only in the end does the novel reveal her name: Felice. Were the novel more structured, it would collapse under the weight of this symbolic quest for happiness. But, as is true of its protagonist, the novel's attention is easily distracted. It takes its readers to bars, speakeasies, and buffet flats, which were private apartments that offered food, liquor, music, and sex. The characters mainly drink, dance, smoke dope, and copulate.

Ray, a Haitian-born intellectual, atheist, and reluctant race man ("Why should we have and love a race?") stands apart. He meets up with Jake on a train, and they travel together for the last two-thirds of the novel. The novel constantly plays up the contrast between them. An inveterate reader and aspiring writer, Ray is strongly anticolonialist, although he feels helpless to affect events. Unlike the charismatic Jake, Ray fails with women, and his experiment with drugs lands him in the hospital. He rues the fact that he is unable to be the "natural man" that Jake is; his intellect and bourgeois morality inhibit him. The idea that intellect gets in the way of feeling was at the heart of the primitivism that gained broad credence during the 1920s. Blacks, free of the inhibitions of civilization, had direct access to feelings, while whites were repressed by their intellects and consciences. McKay was not alone among black writers to try to glean something positive from primitivism. But, like others who tried, he ended up reinforcing stereotypes that were all too prevalent.

In an infamous review in the *Crisis*, W. E. B. Du Bois wrote that after reading *Home to Harlem*, he felt "distinctly like taking a bath." He abhorred the representations of what he called the "debauched Tenth"—the antithesis of the Talented Tenth, the educated elite, that he had identified in *The Souls of Black Folk* as the vanguard of progress. Ray is the only educated character in

McKay's novel, and he eschews the benefits of education. Du Bois missed the fact that Jake, a veteran, is gainfully employed throughout much of the book. As McKay wrote to Weldon Johnson, "I consider this book a real proletarian novel, but I don't expect the nice radicals to see that it is." They did not. For Du Bois and others, *Home to Harlem* was not the positive propaganda that would advance the race.

Racial progress is hardly the point of *Home to Harlem*. It is an experimental novel that attempts to render the jazz-inflected life of Harlem in prose. Music is the backdrop for the situations that offended Du Bois. McKay represents jazz performance in its multiple dimensions: the voice, the instrument, and the dance. His narrator frequently calls out jazz players, much as a bandleader would: he asks readers to listen for the saxophone, the piano, the drums. He works to represent the impact of the music on the body. Consider this description of a performance in the Congo, Jake's favorite Harlem speakeasy:

> They danced, Rose and the boy. Oh, they danced! An exercise of rhythmical exactness for two. There was no motion she made that he did not imitate. They reared and pranced together, smacking palm against palm, working knee between knee, grinning with real joy. They shimmied breast to breast, bent themselves far back and shimmied again. Lifting high her short skirt and showing her green bloomers, Rose kicked. And in his tight nigger-brown suit, the boy kicked even with her. They were right there together, neither going beyond the other.

The passage captures both the choreography of the dance and the "real joy" that it elicits in the performers. The movement of the passage imitates the movement of the dance. Descriptions of action in the past tense yield to imitations of action in the present tense: "smacking palm again palm" and "working knee between knee." The passage uses repetition, gerunds, and internal rhymes (working, grinning, lifting, kick) to produce the illusion of action. The word "shimmied" conjures a specific dance that was popular during the twenties as well as the rapid movement of the hips and shoulders that the verb denotes. Tellingly, in a novel in which most interactions between male and female characters are laced with misogyny, sarcasm, and violence, the partners in dance achieve equanimity.

The Congo bar was worlds away from the Cotton Club; dance was what they had in common. The popularity of black social dance—the Charleston, Black Bottom, Lindy Hop, and the Stomp—soared during the 1920s. Some of the most popular celebrities in Harlem—Florence Mills and Bill "Bojangles" Robinson, to name two—were dancers.

The desire to represent dance inspired visual artists as well as writers. As a caricaturist, Miguel Covarrubias had an edge: his art depended on exaggerating the human figure and he shaped it in ways that mirrored the dance. Among his "Negro Drawings" (1927) were sketches titled "Flapper," "Strut," and "The Stomp." In the last he drew a couple reminiscent of McKay's dancers. The female figure, clad in a short white dress is leading the male, who is wearing a dark suit, white shirt, and bowler hat. The cane he is carrying becomes an element in the dance. The figures' torsos are elongated and arched. Her head is down, while his is raised, but the legs and arms are positioned at similar angles, creating the impression that he is imitating her movements.

An expanded representation of dance performance came from the Chicago-born painter Archibald Motley, who spent part of the 1920s in Paris, where he began to draw bodies in motion. "Stomp" (1927) depicts a room full of musicians and dancers set against a mauve-colored background. The pianist, trombonist, and banjo player are placed in the lower left-hand corner of the canvas: the brass trombone shines. The black-and-white piano keys create a pattern that is repeated in the black suits and white shirts of the musicians and even in their faces. Dancing couples fill the center of the canvas; some bodies lean into each other, others pull apart. One female figure in a white dress dances rapturously: her hands are raised above her head, while the long strand of pearls she wears are twisted behind her back. Unlike the characters in the Congo bar, all the figures here are stylishly clothed; the female figures wear colorful dresses, cloches, and turbans; their jewelry flashes, and, like the trombone, lights the scene. A solitary male figure, heavy-set and bald-headed, with a broad nose and large mouth, sits on the sofa and observes the scene. His stillness contrasts with the dancers' movement. He models the engagement that the painting invites the reader to share. The painting, however, makes no explicitly political point. But, as Motley must have understood, representing black Americans enjoying the pleasure of each other's company *is* a political act.

The Boston-born poet Helene Johnson, the youngest writer of the Renaissance, set several of her poems in Harlem. The untitled "Poem," set in one of Harlem's most popular vaudeville houses, the Lafayette, is a paean to a banjo-player, "a jazz prince," whose flashing eyes and "patent-leathered" feet are entrancing. His performance conjures "tom-toms," a word about which the speaker acknowledges she knows nothing: "Listen to me, will you, what do I know / About tom-toms?" She just likes the sound of it. A similar impulse is at work in the poem "Bottled," where the speaker ponders the meaning of a bottle of sand on exhibit at the 135th Street Library. The label underneath identifies it as being from the Sahara Desert. The day before the speaker had watched a street dancer, whom she now imagines "dancin' in a jungle" with a spirit that is "bottled" on the streets of Harlem. The colloquial language in these poems as well as the free verse form lightens their mood.

In her "Sonnet to a Negro in Harlem," however, Johnson explores the psychological stakes for those Harlemites who felt anything but at home:

You are disdainful and magnificent
Your perfect body and your pompous gait,
Your dark eyes flashing solemnly with hate;
Small wonder that you are incompetent
To imitate those whom you so despise—

Your shoulders towering high above the throng,
Your head thrown back in rich, barbaric song,
Palm trees and mangoes stretched before your eyes

Johnson's subject's regal bearing reflects both his pride and his disdain for a life that he is unable to master. While the poem emphasizes his physical beauty and the graceful stride with which he moves, it draws attention to his eyes and the "hate" that they express. "Hate" is not an emotion that Harlem's boosters would have acknowledged. For them, Harlem signified progress above everything. But many residents did not share in that success. Whether his pride contributes to his failure is a question the poem raises but does not answer. It suggests instead that his failure is a consequence of his refusal or inability to learn the ways of those he hates.

The poem implies that the subject would thrive were he at home where palm trees and mangoes flourish, a home where his "rich, barbaric song" could resound. "Barbaric" is a jarring word for readers today, but it was intended to signal a positive racial difference. The poem's strength is its insight into the subject's alienation. The line, "Let others toil and sweat for labor's sake," does not reinforce the stereotype of blacks' laziness. It explains instead that what might appear to be laziness to the undiscerning eye is, in reality, resistance. The subject refuses to play the part society assigns. Were he to adopt the mantra of the enterprising New Negro, the poem suggests, it would be in vain: "Scorn will efface each footprint that you make." The subject's contemptuous attitude is not simply admirable, it is heroic. That heroism makes him a deserving subject. He refuses to be defeated, and the speaker rejoices in his spirit. The poem concludes: "I love your laughter, arrogant and bold. / You are too splendid for this city street."

Many dreams died, or were deferred, on the streets of Harlem. Mindful of its disappointments, its poets and writers would imagine homes where dreams could be realized. Some, like Helene Johnson, would find that Africa stirred their imaginations. Few had seen it, and little reliable information existed about it, but writers and ordinary folk alike wondered what it meant for them.

Chapter 4
What is Africa to me?

What is Africa to me:
Copper sun, scarlet sea,
Jungle star and jungle track,
Strong bronzed men and regal black
Women from whose loins I sprang
When the birds of Eden sang?
One three centuries removed
From the scenes his fathers loved
Spicy grove, cinnamon tree
What is Africa to me?

Countee Cullen's 1925 poem "Heritage" asks a question that resonated
in the hearts and minds of many black Americans during the
Harlem Renaissance. They knew little about Africa—either its
history or its social complexities, which scholars had yet to
document—but they felt that they were somehow related to it.
Few of the writers had firsthand knowledge of Africa: only
W. E. B. Du Bois, Jessie Fauset, Langston Hughes, and Claude
McKay had set foot on the continent, and Fauset and McKay had
been only to northern Africa. The relationship of blacks in
America to the land of their ancestors could only be imagined.
Some writers like Cullen, who traveled to Morocco after he wrote
"Heritage," drew an idealized homeland that they wished they had

known. They represented themselves as descendants of "strong bronzed men and regal black / women" who had lived in a lost Eden. But their relationship to these ancestors is uncertain at best. On the one hand the African heritage is too distant to be understood. "Africa?" the speaker asks and then answers his own question: "A book one thumbs / Listlessly, till slumber comes." But at other times, the connection feels so intense that the speaker cannot sleep. The images the poem invokes are mainly of flora and fauna. The only individual human figures are "jungle lovers" whose sensual abandon is not at all consistent with the strict codes governing sexual behavior in traditional African societies. But the poem betrays no knowledge of actual Africa. In the end its central concern is not history but spirituality. The speaker ponders his Christian faith, as he asserts that slavery was the price his people paid for Christianity, and wishes that like his pre-Christian ancestors, he served gods who looked like him.

Writers were not the only ones imagining Africa. Painters and sculptors were, however, less interested in representing Africa than in drawing on its artistic traditions. They knew that modernist masters—including Pablo Picasso, Henri Matisse, and Amedeo Modigliani—had been inspired by the African masks they studied in *Le Musée de l'Homme* in Paris. The encounter with the art of Africa was revolutionizing European art. Alain Locke in *The New Negro* averred that black Americans were "acting as the advance-guard of the African peoples in their contact with Twentieth Century civilization." With no consciousness of his own hubris, he spoke of black Americans' mission to rehabilitate the race in world esteem. More politically minded thinkers analyzed the role blacks in the New World could play in the liberation of Africa. Du Bois organized and led Pan-African Congresses in 1919, 1921, 1923, and 1927, where American blacks met with their peers from West Africa and the Caribbean. Finally, hundreds of thousands of blacks in the United States and throughout the African diaspora joined Garvey's UNIA. Garvey, whose mantra was Africa for the Africans, urged his followers to come together from across the world to build a great nation in Africa. His was "the Dream of a Negro Empire."

Marcus Garvey's Africa was unarguably popular and in some ways no less unrealistic than that imagined by the intellectuals who disdained it. He imagined an Africa that was powerful enough to protect people of African descent wherever in the world they were. Unlike the New Negro leaders, he had no hope that racial equality could be achieved in the United States. Insisting that never in history had slaves ruled their former masters, he concluded that the best Negroes could aspire to was token participation in the political processes of the United States. He did not, however, believe that all blacks should go back to Africa, though that is what many who heard him speak thought he meant. He wanted instead to strengthen the political and commercial ties between blacks in the New World and on the African continent. But he first needed to create a Pan-Africanist consciousness. A riveting orator, he sought to instill that consciousness in his audiences. He wove together biblical allusions ("Ethiopia shall stretch forth her hands unto God"), political commentary ("The political readjustment of the world means that those who are not sufficiently able, not sufficiently prepared, will be at the mercy of the organized classes for another one or two hundred years"), and race pride ("When Europe was inhabited by a race of cannibals, a race of savages, naked men, heathens and pagans, Africa was peopled with a race of cultured black men, who were masters of art, science and literature, men who were cultured and refined; men who, it was said, were like the gods.... Why, then, should we lose hope? Black men you were great; you shall be great again.").

Marcus Mosiah Garvey organized the first black mass movement. The odds against this achievement cannot be overstated; for one, it happened without the benefit of mass communication. Garvey had only his voice and his pen. Born in Jamaica in 1887, he had neither wealth nor family connections. When he left the hamlet of St. Ann's Bay, he went to the capital, Kingston, where he found work as a printer's apprentice. He then traveled for work throughout Central and South America—Costa Rica, Panama, Ecuador, Nicaragua, Honduras, Columbia, and Venezuela—and came to the conclusion that black people everywhere faced the common enemies of colonization and exploitation. After spending time in London, where he met like-minded Africans and West Indians, he founded the UNIA in Jamaica in 1914. Garvey's political perspectives were bold, but his economic principles were conservative. He immigrated to the United States in the hope that he could study at Tuskegee Institute because he admired Booker T. Washington's principles of economic self-sufficiency; Garvey planned to establish a school in Jamaica that would propound them. But Washington died shortly after Garvey arrived in the United States. Forced to develop an alternative plan, he moved to New York City and became a leader with whom to reckon: "I asked: where is the black man's government? Where is his king and kingdom? Where is his President, his country, and his ambassador, his army, his navy, his men of big affairs? I could not find them, and then, declared, I will help to make them."

One could say that Harlem enabled Garvey to reinvent himself in ways that allowed him to pursue his grand ambitions. He established his headquarters, Liberty Hall, on West 138th Street in 1917. Within two months, the UNIA had two thousand members. By 1919, the year of "Red Summer," Garvey claimed two million members worldwide. The number is doubtless inflated, but many more people shared parts of Garvey's vision than actually joined his organization. Still, in 1926, the UNIA boasted 725 branches in the United States, most of them in the South, as well as branches in the West Indies, Central and South America, and Africa. The Harlem branch was by far the largest.

For new arrivals in the city, who felt bereft of family and home, the UNIA provided community. Initially, the UNIA resembled traditional fraternal organizations. It promised to provide sickness and death benefits to its members. Its various auxiliaries including

7. The Universal Negro Improvement Association (UNIA) organized massive parades in Harlem, such as this one in 1920, that exemplified founder Marcus Garvey's belief in race pride and race unity.

the African Legion, the Black Star Nurses, and the Royal African Guard, each with distinctive uniforms and regalia, fostered a sense of belonging to those who joined. The organization's parades were beloved in Harlem (fig. 7). Behind the marching auxiliaries, Garvey, resplendent in uniform and plumed helmet, rode in an open car. The UNIA conventions were decidedly grand. In 1920, for example, the month-long international conference ended with Garvey's speech in Madison Square Garden before a crowd of 25,000. The convention designated Garvey as the Provisional President-General of the African Republic, which was deemed a "government in exile." His assistants were given titles such as the Supreme Potentate and the Supreme Deputy Potentate, titles that gave more impetus to critics who mocked Garvey's pomposity.

In 1918 Garvey had founded *Negro World*, which quickly became one of the leading Negro weeklies with a circulation estimated at between 60,000 and 200,000 at the height of its popularity in the early twenties; it continued publication until 1933. The newspaper circulated worldwide until it was banned by colonial governments, possibly because it reported events in Africa, the Caribbean, and Europe as well as in the United States. Every issue included an editorial by Garvey as well as articles expounding his ideas and philosophy. The latter frequently referred in vivid terms to the glorious African past and to New World slave rebellions. Unlike other black-owned newspapers, *Negro World* refused to run ads for the skin lighteners and hair straighteners that were financial mainstays of the Negro press.

Fellow Jamaican Claude McKay criticized Garvey's vision as utopian fantasy. But his sonnet "Africa" explored one of Garvey's favorite themes: the ancient glory of the motherland. It begins, "The sun sought thy dim bed and brought forth light, / The sciences were sucklings at thy breast." These lines call to mind one of Garvey's favorite ripostes: Africa was a site of learning at the time that Europe was in the Dark Ages. But the images of pyramids and the Sphinx conjured ancient Egypt, rather than the West African empires of Mali, Songhai, and Ghana. McKay was hardly alone. Black Americans had claimed the heritage of ancient Egypt, at least as early as David Walker's *Appeal*, the abolitionist document published in 1829. They insisted that Egypt was a part of Africa in response to the insistence of white Americans that it was not. Obviously, blacks had the better argument geographically, but the historical connection was debatable. Nevertheless, much of the iconography of Africa in the New Negro magazines was actually Egyptian iconography: the Sphinx, the pyramids, and figures clothed in Egyptian dress. Tellingly, McKay's poem, published in 1921, extolls Africa as both an "ancient treasure-land" and a "modern prize"—a timely reference to the European scramble for colonies in Africa before and after World War I.

The most important writer in the UNIA was its founder, Marcus Garvey. His prophetic language was hardly modern, but its timeless quality was part of its appeal. "No one knows when the hour of Africa's redemption cometh," he wrote, "It is in the wind. It is coming. One day, like a storm, it will be here. When that day comes all Africa will stand together." The biblical cadence invested Garvey's words with authority. His readers became believers.

Garvey was a visionary who made the mistake of trying to materialize his visions. He established the Negro Factories Corporation, whose purpose was "to build and operate factories in the big industrial centers of the United States, Central America, the West Indies, and Africa to manufacture every marketable commodity." It organized grocery stores, a restaurant, a laundry, and a publishing house, but its successes were modest. The Black Star Line (BSL) was the most audacious of the UNIA enterprises. At a time when shipping was the mode of international transportation, Garvey decided to enter the industry. Its very name, Black Star Line, was intended to suggest some competition with the Cunard's White Star Line, the industry leader. The BSL was also to be a commercial enterprise, intended to link New York and the West Indies, and this move seemed to literalize the promise of "Back to Africa." Capitalized at half a million dollars, it offered shares at $5.00 each. Shares were offered only to blacks, and no individual could purchase more than two hundred shares. The rationale was that even the poorest Negro could become a shareholder. In short order the company raised three-quarters of a million dollars by selling shares to more than forty thousand people. Garvey's critics ridiculed his plan. They were temporarily silenced when he announced the purchase of ships, which Garvey christened with characteristic flair, the SS *Phillis Wheatley* and the SS *Booker T. Washington*. Nonetheless, the BSL enterprise failed: Garvey knew a lot about motivation and salesmanship, but he knew nothing about ships. The men he hired proved either incompetent or untrustworthy or both.

In 1922, the federal government indicted Garvey on charges of mail fraud in connection with the sale of BSL stock. He was convicted, as he was a second time on charges of income tax evasion (on a salary he never received) and was jailed in Atlanta. Although he was pardoned, he was deported to Jamaica in 1927.

By then, Garvey's efforts to materialize his vision by buying land in Liberia had been stymied by the government there. Moreover, his 1923 meeting with leaders of the Ku Klux Klan, based on their shared belief in racial purity, had persuaded Negro leaders that Garvey did not understand U.S. history and politics. The UNIA continued to exist but only as a shadow of its former self.

Like Garvey, W. E. B. Du Bois believed in "Africa for the Africans," arguing that such was the logical inference of President Wilson's declarations that the war had made the world safe for democracy and all people were entitled to self-determination. Despite their shared Pan-Africanist perspectives, Du Bois and Garvey could not make common cause, a failure that is understandable but regrettable. Du Bois disdained Garvey's flamboyant style and penchant for self-aggrandizement. The more popular Garvey became, the more Du Bois considered him a threat to the cause of racial advancement. In the May 1924 issue of the *Crisis*, just after Garvey's mail fraud conviction, Du Bois declared, "Marcus Garvey is, without doubt, the most dangerous enemy of the Negro race in America and in the world. He is either a lunatic or a traitor." Garvey believed that Du Bois was conspiring against him. He also viewed the light-skinned New Englander though the lens of Jamaica's tripartite social system, in which mulattoes enjoyed officially sanctioned privileges. In the United States, however, all Negroes, regardless of complexion, were officially second-class citizens. For his part, Du Bois expressed prejudices against Garvey as a dark-skinned West Indian. Their mutual name-calling was a discredit to both.

Du Bois had an informed critique and a cosmopolitan experience of the world, but he could not excite the masses as Garvey did. Instead of large-scale conventions, Du Bois organized Pan-Africanist Congresses that brought together members of the intellectual elite from throughout the African Diaspora. The mission was to realize "the world-old dream of human brotherhood." The political goal was to free African people from the shackles of colonialism. Representatives from throughout the African diaspora as well as sympathetic whites met to plan long-range strategies and to mount an immediate propaganda campaign. The fact that the meetings were held in the European capitals of London, Brussels, and Paris suggested how distant the goal of political autonomy remained.

In his contribution to Locke's *The New Negro*, "The Negro Mind Reaches Out," Du Bois argued that the ideal of democracy would never be achieved in Europe as long as it was denied in the colonies that "shadowed" the imperial powers. The essay offers both a comprehensive overview and anecdotes drawn from Du Bois's experience. "Modern imperialism and modern industrialism are one and the same system," he insists before detailing examples from Egypt ("Egypt too is Africa") to South Africa, and Sierra Leone to Kenya. He revisits his dictum "the problem of the twentieth century is the problem of the color line," first expressed in 1899 and made famous in *The Souls of Black Folk*, published in 1903. He argues that it is still accurate but only if understood as a problem of labor as well as race. But that understanding is elusive. The Africans who attend the Pan-African Congresses too often represent their colonial rulers rather than the colonized masses. At the Pan-African Congress in Brussels, for example, an African born in the Congo but raised in Belgium defends the indefensible cruelty of King Leopold's exploitation of the Congo. At the essay's close, Du Bois writes that "my ship seeks Africa," and he arrives in Liberia, where "political power has tried to resist the power of modern capital." That resistance was vanquished.

Jessie Fauset was one of the few women to attend any of the Pan African Congresses, and her article "Impressions of the Pan-African Conference," drawn from her notes on the 1921 meeting, was published in the *Crisis*. Although it includes a reference to her presentation on the contributions of women to the freedom struggle in the United States, it ends with a declaration that seems to assume the global struggle is gendered male: "All the possibilities of black men are needed to weld together the black men of the world against the day when black and white meet in battle. God grant that when that day comes we shall be so powerful that the enemy will say, 'But behold! These men are our brothers.'" Fauset was deeply interested in Africa, but in part because of her gender it was difficult for her to express that interest. For example, Fauset declined the invitation to translate *Batouala*, the novel by René Maran that was awarded the Prix Goncourt, the most prestigious literary award in France in 1921, just two years after it had been won by Marcel Proust. Born in Martinique, Maran had served as a colonial official in Africa and made Africans the central figures in *Batouala*. Fauset reviewed both the original publication in French and its translation. She judged it "a great novel. It is artistic, overwhelming in its almost cinema-like sharpness of picturization." But she confided to a friend, "If I should translate that book over my name, I'd never be considered 'respectable' again." She did not explain the reasons, but they may well have included the novel's representations of such customs as polygamy and bride price as well as fictive rituals like the "dance of love," which Maran describes as "intoxication." The anticolonial sentiments that Fauset admired were largely confined to the author's preface.

Fauset made her own way to Africa in 1925 and described her sojourn in the essay, "Dark Algiers the White." She explains that "White Algiers" is the epithet the French gave the city to describe its topography: "the city raises white on tiers up the side of a hill, many hills." Dark Algiers presumably refers to its people. Recounting her arrival, Fauset wrote that from its harbor the city offered a vista of brown and black faces, red fezzes, white turbans, white burnouses, and red blanket robes. "All the strangeness and difference of that life, while starting far, far in the interior of Africa yet breaks off so sharply at the southern edge of the Mediterranean, rose instantly to meet us." To Fauset, the images of Algiers were unforgettable, though their meanings were difficult to decipher. Perhaps borrowing from Maran, she develops a cinematic metaphor and skillfully freezes a series of scenes. At one moment a group of men reminds her of Old Testament patriarchs. A couple comes into view and Fauset thinks the silent woman is "like an automaton besides her lord." An old woman looks out above her veil and seems to Fauset the "very savor of the East." Although her descriptions of people can be condescending and even racist, Fauset most often maintains the perspective of respectful outsider. At the least she is sensitive enough to recognize that to the Algerians she is "equally exotic." But Africa is not her home.

Fauset was not a primitivist at heart; Countee Cullen was. His poem "Fruit of the Flower" explores a theme similar to "Heritage" but written in sparer lines. Here the speaker wonders why he has not inherited the "sober, steady ways" of his father, or the "puritan" spirit of his mother. Instead his is a pagan spirit and he, as well as his father, ponders its source:

> My father is a quiet man
> With sober, steady ways;
> For simile, a folded fan;
> His nights are like his days.
>
> My mother's life is puritan,
> No hint of cavalier,
> A pool so calm you're sure it can
> Have little depth to fear.
>
> And yet my father's eyes can boast
> How full his life has been;
> There haunts them yet the languid ghost
> Of some still sacred sin.
>
> And though my mother chants of God,
> And of the mystic river,
> I've seen a bit of checkered sod
> Set all her flesh aquiver.

Why should he deem it pure mischance
A son of his is fain
To do a naked tribal dance
Each time he hears the rain?

Cullen's adoptive father, the Reverend Frederick Cullen, was the
pastor of Salem Methodist Church, a congregation that he had
built from a store-front mission to one of the leading churches in
Harlem. The minister was also active in the NAACP and well
respected in the community. In contrast to the depiction in the
poem, the pastor's nights might well have been different from his
days; the "folded fan" works as a simile for repression as well as it
does for "sober, steady ways." The "some still sacred sin" might
allude to his sexual peccadilloes and suggest Cullen's uncertain
response. Less is known about his adoptive mother, Carolyn
Cullen, who played the piano and sang soprano in the church
choir. The poem does little more than suggest that her religious
faith has not extinguished human desire. The speaker is left to
consider the source of his "wild" or "pagan spirit." The spirit could
be a metaphor for the homosexual identity that the poet could not
acknowledge. What seems more important is that Cullen coded
sexual and spiritual difference in terms of primitivism. His poems
attribute any nonconformist behavior to an atavistic source, which
speaks to the pervasiveness of primitivism in 1920s life. It was a
handy, if deeply problematic, frame of reference.

In "The Legacy of the Ancestral Arts," Alain Locke offered an
arresting counter to the mythology of African primitivism.
Training his eye on African sculpture, he pronounced it "rigid,
controlled, disciplined, abstract, and heavily conventionalized."
It was anything but "primitive," an adjective he considered
appropriate to describe the art of black Americans, their music,
poetry, and dance, which he considered "free, exuberant,
emotional, sentimental, and naïve." Locke enumerated a long list
of European artists who had been influenced by African art. He
cited scholars who attested to the originality of African sculptors,

who "can see form in three dimensions." Locke lamented the absence of a tradition of visual art among black Americans, although he listed all the Negro artists he could. He noted that African sculpture was as alien to them as to their white countrymen. However, were the black American artist to embrace African art, he would recognize that he is "not a cultural foundling without his own inheritance." Here and elsewhere, Locke wants both to claim and deny an essentialist connection between blacks in America and in Africa.

Locke points to the attraction of African sculpture to European painters, which offers them "fresh motifs." But black Americans could derive much more from the study of African art: "a classical background, the lessons of discipline, style, [and] technical control pushed to the limits of technical mastery." They could create art in the tradition of West Africa rather than that of the United States. Not only was the former more distinguished, the latter had deliberately excluded black subjects, despite their presence in American life. Locke notes parenthetically that black figures appear frequently in European painting, even though the black population in Europe was miniscule. He illustrates the essay with diverse images of African sculpture from Benin, Dahomey, Sudan, and the Congo, all of which were held in the collection of Albert Barnes.

Barnes, a physician and chemist who discovered a cure for infant blindness, had already established the foundation that bears his name; the suburban Philadelphia mansion that long housed the foundation was built the same year *The New Negro* was published. Barnes's fortune was as deep as his tastes were eclectic; he amassed one of the largest collections of Impressionist and Post-Impressionist European paintings in the United States as well as an extensive store of African sculptures, which he exhibited for their aesthetic values rather than their ethnographic significance. "Negro Art and America," Barnes's contribution to Locke's anthology, does not discuss his collection or his radical views on art education. In many ways, Barnes's theories on art were fiercely nonhierarchical and democratic. In collaboration with John Dewey, Barnes developed an art curriculum for workers that shaped the offerings at the school run by his foundation. He insisted on displaying his collection without regard to chronology or nationality. A single gallery might hold French paintings, African sculptures, hand-wrought iron, and Pennsylvania Dutch furniture. Despite this practice, his essay inscribes racial hierarchy and relies heavily on the supposed primitivism of Africans and African Americans, people for whom no boundary exists between art and life. Barnes's real contribution to the volume was the reproductions of his art.

Several New Negro artists had already embarked on the path Locke set forth. One that he singles out is Laura Wheeler, who illustrated Fauset's essay, "Dark Algiers the White" for the *Crisis*. Born in Hartford, Connecticut, Wheeler Waring, as she was later known, studied at the Pennsylvania Academy of Fine Arts before joining the faculty at Cheney State Teachers College, a short distance from Philadelphia, where she taught from 1926 until her death. Her portraits of Negro women are particularly notable; the portrait of Ann Washington Derrick won the Harmon Foundation Gold Medal in 1927. Like Fauset, she traveled widely. She made her first trip to Europe and North Africa in 1914 and studied for a year in Paris. Her illustrations appeared frequently in the *Crisis*. The June 1924 cover was titled "Africa in America." It depicts a bejeweled female figure, holding a calabash, looking at a landmass that links the maps of Africa and America. The only object drawn among the swirling lines that make up the map is a sailing ship. The human figure that towers over the ship equals the continents in size. Africa in America is gendered female.

Aaron Douglas was arguably the most successful of the New Negro visual artists as well as the one most dedicated to deploying Africanist techniques. Born and raised in Lincoln, Nebraska, Douglas arrived in Harlem in 1925 and left four years later. By that time, his images were everywhere. Most people who knew his work encountered it in the *Crisis* and *Opportunity* or on the book jackets he illustrated. These included Cullen's anthology, *Caroling Dusk* (1927); Langston Hughes's *Fine Clothes to the Jew* (1927); James Weldon Johnson's *The Autobiography of an Ex-Colored Man* (1927) and *God's Trombones* (1927); and Claude McKay's *Banjo* (1928), *Banana Bottom* (1929), *Home to Harlem* (1928), and *A Long Way from Home* (1937). Sympathetic to the goals of the younger writers, Douglas was also the artist of the cover of the November 1926 issue of *Fire!!*, the brilliant but short-lived literary journal.

Although Douglas painted realistic portraits and used impressionist techniques to paint buildings such as a power plant in Harlem, he was compelled by such subjects as Negro history, mythology, and spirituality, which were difficult to represent. The principles of abstract design that characterized African art were suited to his purpose. In his illustrations for *God's Trombones*, a series of poems inspired by folk sermons, Douglas takes his cue from Bible stories such as Noah and the Ark, the Prodigal Son, and the Crucifixion. Originally painted in muted tones, the illustrations were reproduced in black and white. The two-dimensional paintings feature black subjects whose features are abstracted and resemble African masks. The central figure in *The Crucifixion* is Simon the Cyrenian, a man believed to be black, who was ordered by the Romans to carry the cross for Christ up the mountain of Golgotha. (Simon the Cyrenian is also the subject of a poem by Countee Cullen.) The figure's posture and open mouth suggest the arduousness of the burden. More important, the figure's long limbs and the cross itself create asymmetrical planes and angles that focus the viewer's eye. A series of concentric circles in varying shades of purple and mauve draws attention to the figures of a haloed Christ and three disciples. Yet these seemingly illuminated figures are not the painting's focus; they are dwarfed by the figure of Simon, a hero that the painting seeks to reclaim.

The murals Douglas painted for the 135th Street Library, *Aspects of Negro Life*, repeat elements found in *The Crucifixion*. Muted palettes, abstract figures, and an overall focus on design characterize these paintings; their size and subject are epic. Some as large as six feet x six feet trace black American history from Africa through slavery and Reconstruction to the industrial North. Much of this history is characterized by exploitation and violent oppression. The first panel, *The Negro in an African Setting*, tells a different story. The mural centers a pair of dancers in motion, each leaning backward with one leg curved and lifted off the ground. The male figure holds a spear in one hand and an assegai in the other. A small carving, perhaps a symbol of ancestry, is placed upon the heads of the couple. Figures with spears fill the canvas. The dancers' ankle and leg bands are repeated on these figures as well as on the drummers who are placed in the foreground of the painting.

Music and dance are crucial elements in all of the murals. They forge the spiritual connection between people of African descent in Africa and the New World. African drummers are replaced by banjo players in the ironically titled *Idyll of the Deep South*, which depicts figures working in the fields. In *From Slavery to Reconstruction*, figures pick cotton at the left of the panel, while a trumpeter plays on the right. Soldiers and worshippers fill the frame. But the central figure is a speaker, book in hand, whose finger is pointing upward. The final panel (fig. 8) is titled *Song of the Towers*. It evokes the Great Migration and the persistent exploitation of black labor.

Ironically, Douglas's most influential teacher was the German-born Winhold Reiss, himself a student of African art, who designed the cover, decorative features, and illustrations of *The New Negro*. One could say that Douglas's learning about African art from a European teacher was a microcosm of the larger impact of the discovery of African art by European painters. Douglas studied African sculpture not in a Paris museum but in the

8. Painter Aaron Douglas and Schomburg Collection founder and curator Arthur A. Schomburg stand in front of Douglas's mural, *Aspects of Negro Life: Song of the Towers*, at the Schomburg Center in New York. It uses techniques inspired by African art to depict twentieth-century African American life.

collection of Albert Barnes, which also included paintings of emerging European modernists. Douglas exemplified Locke's understanding that black Americans had to *learn* about African art; it was not an intuitive connection.

Years before Langston Hughes traveled to Africa, he captured lyrically the connection between blacks in the United States and Africa in the poem "The Negro Speaks of Rivers." For Hughes the connection was more spiritual and historical than political:

> I've known rivers.
> I've known rivers ancient as the world and older than the flow
>   of human blood
> in human veins.
>
> My soul has grown deep like the rivers.
>
> I bathed in the Euphrates when dawns were young.
> I built my hut near the Congo and it lulled me to sleep.
> I looked upon the Nile and raised the pyramids above it.
> I heard the singing of the Mississippi when Abe Lincoln
> went down to New Orleans, and I've seen its muddy
> bosom turn all golden in the sunset.
> I've known rivers:
> Ancient dusky rivers.
>
> My soul has grown deep like the rivers.

The poem captures the majesty of the spirituals, as it employs one of that genre's key tropes—the river. "Deep River," "One More River to Cross," "Roll, Jordan Roll," and "O, Wasn't That a Wide River" are a few of the songs that use the central metaphor that Hughes adopts. Continuity and timelessness are qualities associated with rivers that the poem attributes to the race, here embodied in the collective "I" of the poem. That "I" is also a common element in the spirituals, as is the use of a refrain. The repetition of "I've known" intensifies the impact of the statement. At a time when the social consensus held that blacks had no heritage, the poem associates blacks with other key sites in human history. The Tigris-Euphrates valley was then considered the cradle of civilization. The poem connects the Negro both to the Congo and the Nile. As Du Bois did in his essay, Hughes in his poem reminds readers that Egypt is indeed in Africa. The poem links fabled African rivers with the most fabled river in the United States, the Mississippi, a major artery of the slave trade. Rather than the fear that enslaved people had of being sold "down the Mississippi," the poem references Abe Lincoln, traveling south to New Orleans; the hope embodied in Lincoln is imaged as the transformation of the muddy Mississippi turning "all golden in the sunset." The poem's implicit assertion is that if the history of blacks arcs back to antiquity, the future of blacks stretches equally far.

Hughes embarked on his African journey in 1923. He sailed on a steamer that dropped anchor in Dakar, Lagos, Accra, and Freetown, as well as in ports in Angola and the Congo. Although in *The Big Sea* he wrote mainly about six months aboard the ship rather than in port, Hughes retained an interest in the people, literature, and politics of the continent throughout his life. But this maiden voyage left only a slight imprint on his writing. His poem, "Afro-American Fragment," published in the *Crisis* in 1930 suggests one possible reason:

So long
So far away
Is Africa.
Not even memories alive
Save those that songs
Beat back into the blood—
Beat out of blood with words sad-sung
In strange un-Negro tongue—
So long,
So far away
Is Africa.

The poem echoes Cullen's "Heritage" in its representation of the ineffable distance, across both time and space, between "Afro-Americans" and their homeland. After acknowledging the distance, the speaker in "Heritage" moves quickly to imagine what his ancestors left behind three centuries before. In fact, most Africans bound for the New World arrived after 1725. The Africa the speaker imagines is equally ahistorical, an Edenic space that has nothing to do with the social and political complexities then confronting a largely colonized continent. For Cullen's speaker, "Africa" is a myth that elicits his spiritual contemplation. Hughes, perhaps because he had seen sub-Saharan Africa—at least the Atlantic ports in which his ship docked—was less willing to traffic in myths. The poem suggests a cultural connection that is conveyed through song, but the connection cannot be translated or fully understood. The poem's speaker recognizes the limits of his knowledge and his imagination, as even the poem's title suggests.

Hughes published little about his African travels, save the short story "Danse Africaine," until he chronicled them in his autobiography, *The Big Sea*, in 1940. In his later life, he made extended trips to nations across the continent. He championed its writers. His pioneering anthology, *An African Treasury: Articles, Essays, Stories, Poems by Black Africans*, was published in 1960.

During the Harlem Renaissance years, however, he found his inspiration closer to home. Along with several of his peers, he journeyed to the American South.

Chapter 5
"Strong roots sink down"

Many Renaissance artists preferred to explore the Negro homeland on this side of the Atlantic. The South, from which so many ordinary people fled, fired artists' imaginations, especially those like Zora Neale Hurston and James Weldon Johnson, both of whom had been born there. Langston Hughes was born in Missouri and grew up in Kansas and Ohio; Hurston would be his guide to the South. The Washington, D.C.–born Jean Toomer was reborn an artist in Georgia. He was captivated by the physical setting—the red clay, pine trees, and sugar cane—and transfixed by what he called the "peculiar quality of dusk" there. The expressive culture of southern black people, the folklore that included stories, sermons, spirituals, work songs, and blues offered writers inspiration and models. These stories and songs were not the work of the educated or the middle class. In Hurston's judgment, "the Negro farthest down" had made the greatest contributions to American culture. Some of her peers had no interest in unlettered rural southerners who seemed left behind in the race to modernity; others wanted to use their lore as raw material for works of literary art. Hurston, however, knew that the richly complex lore could stand on its own. Even so, she conceded that while collecting it, "I picked up glints and gleams out of what I had and stored it away for my own use."

For many writers, the language of rural southerners and of those northern migrants who, like Hurston, had the map of Dixie on their tongues, was even more useful than the folk material. Rich in drama and metaphor, it was as fresh an idiom for literature as African masks were for visual art. In order to use it, however, writers had to strip it of its negative associations with minstrelsy. Minstrel shows were the first popular entertainment in the United States; they featured white men in blackface who acted out stereotypes of black men; performers with exaggerated physical features slouched across the stage, often eating watermelon. Their speech was a caricature of the language black southerners spoke. Minstrel acts were updated for twentieth-century vaudeville, but their odor lingered on the stage.

The influence of minstrelsy was so strong that James Weldon Johnson wrote in his preface to the first edition of *The Book of American Negro Poetry*, published in 1922, that "as an instrument for poetry, dialect has only two main stops, humor and pathos." What Negro poets needed instead was a "form that will express the racial spirit by symbols within rather than by symbols without." What he called the "mutilated spellings" of dialect represented the outward symbols that the writer needed to put down. When Johnson published a second edition of his anthology in 1931, he reached a different conclusion. Although they used racialized language, young writers including Sterling Brown and Langston Hughes had fashioned a new form of poetry out of the "common, racing, living authentic speech of the Negro in certain phases of real life." Those "phases" were the lives of "the Negro farthest down."

Johnson himself was inspired by the figure that he called the "old-time Negro preacher." In the preface to *God's Trombones: Seven Negro Sermons in Verse*, Johnson described him "a master of all the modes of eloquence." He often possessed a voice that was "a marvelous instrument," a voice he could modulate from "a sepulchral whisper to a crashing thunder clap.... He had the power to sweep his hearers before him; and so himself was often swept away. At such times his language was not prose but poetry." The preacher's language was also not dialect, according to Johnson, it was rather a fusion of "Negro idioms" and the language of the King James Bible.

In *God's Trombones*, Johnson's poems are modeled on the preacher's poetry. The title evokes the timbre of the preacher's voice as well his skillful manipulation of his instrument. Most importantly, Johnson experiments with a literary language that would catch the preacher's spirit. Consider "The Creation," the volume's most popular poem. It recounts the events of the opening chapters of Genesis and contains all of the drama that Johnson and, later, Hurston attributed to the old-time preacher:

> Then He stopped and looked and saw
> That the earth was hot and barren.
> So God stepped over to the edge of the world
> And He spat out the seven seas—
> He batted His eyes, and the lightnings flashed—
> He clapped His hands, and the thunders rolled—
> And the waters above the earth came down,
> The cooling waters came down.

The drama inheres in the language, especially the action verbs, and the repetition; the stanza's last line repeats the one above it. Johnson also strived to capture the rhythm of the preacher's language. The syncopation is suggested here by the verbs "stepped" and "clapped," actions that the preacher would perform. The poem itself ends with the preacher comparing the Creator to a "mammy," and this seals the poem's representation of an anthropomorphic God, one that is loving rather than vengeful. The poem allows the inference that the man who is created out of the dust and clay is black. Although he seemingly lacks a political agenda, Johnson's preacher makes a profoundly political statement about the humanity of black people. *God's Trombones* is one of the few books by Harlem Renaissance writers that has never gone out of print. It found its audience in the preachers and their congregations whose words and rituals inspired it. Preachers used the volume not as a text to be preached but as a musical score around which they could improvise new sermons.

By the 1920s, two generations of Negroes had done everything in their power to erase the memories of their ancestors' enslavement. To some, the Negro spirituals—which in 1903 W. E. B. Du Bois deemed "the most beautiful human expression borne this side the seas"—represented that past. Then artists and intellectuals, building on Du Bois's statement, revised their understanding of this body of sacred music. Du Bois responded to the words of the songs, the metaphors of rocks, mountains, and wilderness, as well as "the eloquent omissions and silences." They sang of mothers and children, but not fathers, and never of home except as a deferred destination. Not only were the lyrics haunting, they registered a protest of the singers' condition. Whether explicitly in "O Freedom" and "Go Down, Moses" or implicitly in "Steal Away" and "Swing Low, Sweet Chariot," the songs expressed a will to be free. Many middle-class congregations refused to sing them nonetheless; they preferred songs from white Protestant hymn books to songs associated with slavery.

Alain Locke was less interested in the social interpretation of the spirituals than in the quality of the music: its "utter distinctiveness of the melodic, harmonic, and rhythmic elements." He held that spirituals in the 1920s were in a transitional stage between folk art and art form. He cited the young classically trained musicians— Nathaniel Dett, Edward Boatner, Lawrence Brown, and Hall Johnson—whose arrangements were sung by Negro college choirs. Locke predicted that composers would tap in the "rich vein of this new musical ore," not so much to preserve the legacy of the spirituals as to develop it into a modernist musical form.

Roland Hayes and Marian Anderson, both of whom came to fame in the decade as recitalists, mainly sang Italian arias and German lieder, but began to add a selection of spirituals at the end of their concerts. Paul Robeson made a more dramatic choice: he sang a recital consisting entirely of spirituals in April 1925 in a Greenwich Village theater. By then Robeson was well known as a football star at Rutgers, a Columbia University law student, and an actor who starred in Eugene O'Neill's plays *All God's Chillun Got Wings* and *The Emperor Jones*. Not classically trained, Robeson reflected that he had "unconsciously absorbed the manner of singing spirituals as they should be sung," as he grew up in the small-town churches pastored by his father. At the New York concert, he sang "I Got a Home in Dat Rock," "Joshua Fit de Battle ob Jericho," and "Steal Away," songs that would remain in his repertoire for the rest of his life. Robeson understood that spirituals were not a solo music. His accompanist, Lawrence Brown, sometimes added his voice as well as his piano to produce the call-and-response pattern that was central to the communal performance of spirituals.

Robeson's efforts notwithstanding, Zora Neale Hurston declared, "there never has been a presentation of genuine Negro spirituals to an audience anywhere," in her essay "Spirituals and Neo-Spirituals." Her point was that spirituals were sung by congregations; they were not sung by soloists or quartets. Even when college or professional choirs performed, they sang neo-spirituals that were "arranged" and sung note-for-note according to the arranger's notation. By contrast, the "people," in Hurston's description, sang as the spirit moved them. The "jagged harmonies" they produced were critical to the genre of spirituals. Furthermore, Hurston observed, "the congregation is bound by no rules. No two times singing is alike, so we must consider the rendition of a song not as the final thing, but as a mood. It won't be the same thing next Sunday."

Several writers were moved by the power of both the spirituals and neo-spirituals, and incorporated their motifs and metaphors in modernist poetry and prose. Langston Hughes's "The Negro

Speaks of Rivers" is one example; Jean Toomer's *Cane* offers several more. In "Song of the Son," the central poem in *Cane* the speaker makes a journey to the South in order to gain a usable past. Believing that vestiges of that past are disappearing, he represents himself as arriving just in time to still hear the voices: "Caroling softly souls of slavery / What they were and what they are to me / Caroling softly souls of slavery."

Jean Toomer created a distinctive literary language that fused southern black vernacular and poetic diction in *Cane*. Its form is equally distinctive: a mélange of poetry and prose, lyrical portraits of black women in Georgia, short stories, and an experimental drama. Recurrent themes of alienation, exploitation, and fragmentation unify the volume as do repeated metaphors of sugar cane, dusk, red clay, and pine trees.

The first section of *Cane* limns portraits of women, whose physical beauty is irresistible to the men who exploit them and whose spirituality is unfulfilled by the fundamentalist Christianity that is their only outlet. A lyrical refrain opens the book: "Her skin is like dusk on the eastern horizon / O cant you see it, O cant you see it / Her skin is like dusk on the eastern horizon / …When the sun goes down." Karintha is the twelve-year-old child whose beauty is invisible to the white world but all too alluring to black men, young and old, who vie for her sexual favors. They do not care that the "soul of her was a thing ripened too soon." Karma is a woman, strong as a man, who betrays her husband who is sentenced to the chain gang. Becky is a white woman who is the mother of two Negro sons. Both whites and blacks treat her like a pariah, yet sneak to bring her food. Religion offers no comfort, even as "the pines whisper to Jesus." Becky dies in a fire and "the Bible flaps its leaves with an aimless rustle on her mound." Perhaps the most memorable of these women is Fern, whose first name reveals her oneness with nature; readers only learn her full name at the conclusion of the sketch: "Fernie May Rosen." Her spirituality is palpable, but it lacks proper channel for expressions. Her Jewish last name suggests her alienation from the Christian community in which she lives. The narrator is a young northerner who thinks that he can bring her what she needs. But, like the other male figures in the book, he has no clue what that is. When he looks at Fern, "her eyes, unusually weird and open, held me. Held God." He feels as though he is about to have a vision. He does not, but Fern does, and her swaying body mystifies him. "Blood-Burning Moon" introduces the last of these women, Louisa, who is caught between her white lover, Bob Stone, and her black lover, Tom Burrell. The plot is driven by this love triangle, but the setting is at least as intriguing. Toomer depicts the Georgia landscape that both inspired and terrified him: "The full moon in the great door was an omen. Negro women improvised songs against its spell." The songs cannot hold fate at bay. Interracial love can end only in violence.

The second section of *Cane* is set in northern cities—Washington, D.C. and Chicago—but the culture of the South resonates. For example, "a soil-soaked fragrance" comes from one of the spectators in the story "Box Seat." "Through the cement floor her strong roots sink down," the narrator observes, thereby acknowledging the many black migrants who stayed connected to their southern roots. Their speech, music, and dance reflected the connections. At the same time, the mores of southern whites, especially their disdain for interracial relationships (at least public ones) migrated northward as well. "Bona and Paul," a story set in Chicago, explores the social and psychological barriers that thwart the relationship between its two title characters; Bona is a white woman, and Paul is rumored to have a mixed-race identity.

The drama "Kabnis" closes the volume. Ralph Kabnis is a northern-born black who, as Toomer had, comes south to teach in a conservative school. He hates its rules: teachers can neither smoke nor drink. He is, however, compelled by the beauty of the surrounding landscape. At the same time, the horror of lynching and other forms of southern racism, the overwhelming poverty of blacks, and elements of their expressive culture repel Kabnis. Yet, he realizes, the beauty and ugliness of the South are inextricably bound. A poet, he does not fit in with the local blacks. They in turn play on his fears, his questions go unanswered. In the end he believes that only Father John, a blind former slave, could answer them. But Father John's answers are a riddle to Kabnis. The theme of "Kabnis" restates a theme of the entire volume: the question of Negro identity can be answered only by confronting the history of slavery and its aftermath.

Toomer's fusion of folk idiom and modernist elements was a revelation to his fellow writers. Readers were not impressed; *Cane* sold fewer than five hundred copies. Experimental writing has never been popular. The elements that initially put readers off became conventional across the twentieth century, and today's audiences find *Cane* accessible. At its publication, it earned effusive praise from Langston Hughes, Weldon Johnson, and Wallace Thurman. Its influence can be traced in the writings of Sterling Brown and Zora Neale Hurston.

Hughes and Brown were drawn to the blues and the ballad that led them to invent new forms of poetry. Having grown up hearing the country blues, then becoming an aficionado of the classic blues, Hughes invented the genre of blues poetry. Some of his poems follow the twelve-bar blues formula: three lines, the second repeating the first with occasional variation, and the third completing the thought and clinching the rhyme. As a writer, Hughes could not deploy the tools that the singers had at their disposal: vocal timbre, gesticulation, and instrumental accompaniment. Neither could he pull from the audience's response, as singers regularly did in performance. He had only the words on the page. Yet Hughes could enact a performance of his own. Consider the opening stanza of "Young Gal's Blues":

I'm gonna walk to the graveyard
'Hind my friend Miss Cora Lee
Gonna walk to the graveyard

'Hind my dear friend Cora Lee
Cause when I'm dead some
Body'll have to walk behind me.

The poem represents the intrusion of death on a young woman's life, a not uncommon theme in the blues. Death is intrusive, but not unexpected; the speaker accepts the prospect of her own death with equanimity. In the meantime she pays respects to her friend. The first-person speaker's determination is reinforced by repetition, typical of the blues, and by her colloquial speech: "gonna" expresses more resolve than the grammatically correct "I'm going to." The honorific "Miss" tells readers something about Cora Lee, because black women had to fight to be addressed with the respect the title accorded. Having fought for respect in life, she has earned respect in death. Hughes uses the twelve-bar blues formula, though he doubles the lines. The slight variation between the first and second statement adheres to the formula.

The poem continues for four stanzas. Rather than a sustained narrative, it produces a series of associative fragments that represent the speaker's consciousness. She thinks of her aunt relegated to a poorhouse and reflects on the trade-off between an early death and a long life marked by poverty and the ugliness of aging. At the end of the poem, she is left with questions and a baseless hope that her man will continue to love her.

"Hard Daddy" might be read as a follow-up to "Young Gal's Blues." When the speaker informs her love she has the blues, he responds, "can't you bring me no better news?" She cries, but he offers no sympathy. In contrast to the earlier poem, this speaker not only longs for escape but for retribution:

I wish I had wings to
Fly like the eagle flies
I wish I had wings to
Fly like the eagle flies

> I'd fly on ma man an'
> I'd scratch out both his eyes.

The metaphor of flight is associated more with black American sacred music than with the secular blues. But rather than the spiritual transcendence expressed in such songs as "If I Had Two Wings to Veil My Face," "I'll Fly Away," and "Ride the Chariot," the hope here is for the all-too-human revenge. This speaker is not yearning for the afterlife, and she recognizes that she can only dream of revenge; in the end she will not achieve it.

While teaching in Lynchburg, Virginia, Sterling Brown spent his spare time traveling the countryside and documenting the songs and stories he heard. One of his poems, "Odyssey of Big Boy," puts the heroic mantle of Odysseus on a black laborer. Another, "Southern Road," re-creates the rhythmic meter of a work song. A trickster hero, "Slim Greer," is the subject of a cycle of poems set variously in Arkansas, Atlanta, and Hell. Brown, like Hughes, wrote blues poems, but his were set in the rural South, as the title "Tin Roof Blues" suggests.

One of Brown's most enduring poems is "Ma Rainey." It depicts this "Mother of the Blues" in a performance at a tent show, far from the glamour of city life. The towns the poem names, Cape Girardeau and Poplar Bluff, identify the setting as rural Missouri, while references to New Orleans and Mobile suggest that events like this one occur across the South. Rainey's audience arrives by automobile, mule, and train: "Comes flivverin' in, / Or ridin' mules / Or packed in trains / Picknickin' fools." Their sense of expectation is palpable. The second stanza is written in the same vernacular language as the first, but its lines are elongated: they specify the backgrounds of the spectators (river settlements, black bottoms, and lumber camps) and describe their behavior (laughing, cheering, and waiting for their "aches and miseries" to be assuaged) as they enter the performance space. The third stanza invokes the singer's power:

O Ma Rainey,
Sing yo' song:
Now you's back
Whah you belong,
Git way inside us,
Keep us strong...
O Ma Rainey,
Li'l an' low,
Sing us 'bout de hard luck
Roun' our do';
Sing us 'about de lonesome road
We mus' go...

The poem affirms the spiritual power of the blues. Ma Rainey acts as a priestess who ministers to her audience. To be sure, she is one with them, but she has a gift that they do not have. Her song has the power to revive her audience, and this is no small irony by reminding them of the harsh realities of their lives. The two ellipses in this stanza seem to suggest that no end is in sight for their troubles, but their strength is ongoing as well.

In the final stanza, the poem turns the spotlight on Rainey, who sings "Backwater Blues," a song Rainey introduced that was later made even more famous by her student Bessie Smith. The poem quotes the song, which thereby becomes a structural element in the poem. The speaker, who now seems something of an outsider, converses with an insider. That "fellow's" judgment stands as the poem's final statement: "She jes' gits hold of us dataway." The effect of Rainey's art cannot be denied but neither can it be fully explained.

Brown continued to be drawn to the music. As it was for Hughes, the music was a source not only of inspiration but a source for the formal elements that structured his poems. "Strong Men," for example, represents the capacity of a range of musical genres— spirituals, work songs, and blues—to reflect, critique, and encourage the community of people who created them. Its stanzas alternate between Whitmanesque free verse, which recounts the history of blacks in America, and stanzas in the form of musical quotations, which capture the response to the call of history. It charts an increasing militant spirit that grows from "Keep a-inching along like a po' inchworm" to "Me an' muh baby gonna shine" to the poet's own fierce lines: "The strong men...coming on / The strong men gittin' stronger. / Strong men.../ Stronger."

No writer is more identified with the South than Zora Neale Hurston, who was proud to say that she had been born in the cradle of Negro folklore. Although she lied about where and when, she got the main fact correct. Hurston claimed to have been born in the all-black town of Eatonville, Florida. She was in fact born in Notasulga, Alabama, a hamlet not far from Tuskegee Institute (fig. 9). Although she would later claim to have been born in 1901 or 1903, she was born on January 7, 1891. Whether or not she was born in Eatonville, it was her home. Her father, the Reverend John Hurston, was thrice elected mayor of the town. Her mother, Lucy Potts Hurston, always encouraged her fifth child to "jump at the sun," to dream as big as she could. Zora complied. Her imagination was sparked by the "lying sessions," or storytelling, that she overheard on Joe Clarke's store porch, "the heart and spring of the town." In these stories, "God, Devil, Brer Rabbit, Brer Fox, Sis Cat, Brer Lion, Tiger, Buzzard, and all the wood folk walked and talked like natural men."

Hurston had a way of making "a straight lick out of a crooked stick." In the ivied halls of Barnard College, she developed an accurate and insightful view of her past. Through the study of anthropology, she learned to appreciate her Eatonville experiences intellectually as well as intuitively. Her homefolk were part of cultural anthropology, scientific subjects who could be studied for their academic value. Not surprisingly, Hurston's first research expedition took her back to Eatonville, where she tried to write down the stories she had heard as a child. Although her neighbors

9. Writers Jessie Fauset, Langston Hughes, and Zora Neale Hurston pose before the statue of Booker T. Washington at Tuskegee Institute, Tuskegee, Alabama, in 1927. Hughes was traveling in the South for the first time, and Hurston, then beginning her ethnographic fieldwork, intermittently served as his informal guide. Fauset was Hughes's one-time mentor.

did not think that "lies" were important, they acceded to her requests to tell them.

After graduating from Barnard in 1927, Hurston spent five years crisscrossing Florida, braving Louisiana bayous, and visiting Bahamian plantations collecting stories, sermons, and songs to uncover "that which the soul lives by," the practices and beliefs that defined her subjects' interior lives. She knew that those beliefs would be hard to document, for people did not yield their private truths easily. Besides, hoodoo was a set of pre-Christian beliefs and practices that was widely disparaged. Hurston determined, as she would later write, "to *go* there tuh *know* there." Unlike Toomer, she was not in a hurry to capture the vestiges of a dying culture; rather, Hurston was convinced there was a surfeit of material, more than she would ever be able to document. Besides, folklore was being "made and unmade" every day. It would never run out. Hurston believed moreover that she was not collecting raw material that could be refined into art. She believed instead that "folklore was the art a people made before they knew there was such a thing as art."

In her 1934 essay, "Characteristics of Negro Expression," Hurston set forth conclusions she had drawn from her five years in the field. They apply to rural, black, southern culture or, as it were, to the Negro farthest down. The first characteristic is drama: "every phase of Negro life is highly dramatized. Everything is acted out....There is an impromptu ceremony always ready for every hour of life." The second characteristic, "the will to adorn," is the impulse to ornament an ornament, which Hurston identified in the profusion of metaphor and simile that characterized the speech of rural black Americans. She heard it in phrases such as "sobbing hearted," "low-down" and "top superior," and in the use of verbifications such as "funeralize." Hurston simply ignored the then widely held belief that poor Negroes were not capable of speaking standard English: they were deemed either too stupid or, according to some "scholars" of the day, their lips were too thick to enunciate words properly. Hurston simply observed that Negro speech had changed the way southern white men spoke. In the essay "Spirituals and Neo-Spirituals," she declared that "nothing outside of the Old Testament is as rich in figure as a Negro prayer. Some instances are unsurpassed anywhere in literature." She argued that a crucial tenet of black southern culture was the importance of beauty: the feeling that animated everyday speech, not to mention the language of courtship and sacred worship was "there could never be too much of beauty, let alone enough."

That feeling animates Hurston's fiction, as it draws on the language of the folk to invent a distinctive literary language, and indeed it incorporates folklore texts. For example, a sermon she transcribed in the field is used in a pivotal moment in her 1934 novel, *Jonah's Gourd Vine*, set in Eatonville and loosely based on the lives of Hurston's parents. "Wounded in the House of My Friends" is a version of the "train sermon" that Weldon Johnson identified. In this instance, the train begins it journey in the Garden of Eden and goes all the way to Judgment Day. In *Their Eyes Were Watching God*, Hurston interpolates courtship rituals and blues performance as well as the "lying sessions" on Joe Clarke's store porch. As the novel represents it, the porch was a public space reserved for men. Hurston celebrated the wealth of the expressive culture in rural black communities, but she also critiqued the exclusion of women from it.

Delia Jones, the protagonist of Hurston's early short story "Sweat," is a washerwoman, the family breadwinner, and an abused wife who finds her only solace in religion. Her husband, Sykes, is both literally and figuratively a snake charmer, who resents and relies on Delia's money. For the first half of the story, Delia acts meekly as she believes that God will punish Sykes for his meanness, infidelity, and physical cruelty. But when Sykes brings home a rattlesnake to set a trap for Delia, she moves to beat Sykes at his own game. She leaves the house, takes refuge outside, and waits for Sykes to be caught in his own snare. Lines from spirituals thread through the story; in the end it is clear that the faithful Delia will not "cross Jurden in a calm time." In the process of saving her life, she has lost her soul. Hurston would continue to write about marital discord, but she would give her future protagonists better choices than she invented for Delia Jones.

In two of her nonfiction books, *Mules and Men* and *Dust Tracks on a Road*, Hurston describes a woman she met at a lumber camp in Polk County, Florida, who suggested other possibilities. Hurston called her Big Sweet, a name that testified to both her physical strength and her gentleness. This woman could talk tough with anyone who threatened her, whether it was her female rival, her male lover, or the white boss. She could also "talk sweet" with those she cared about, including Hurston. She became Hurston's guide and protector on the job as she was once ready to wield a knife to protect Hurston. Even though Big Sweet did not understand the reasons Hurston wanted to collect "lies," she helped her find the best storytellers; she herself is one of the few female storytellers in *Mules and Men*. With a lucky piece of hoodoo in her hair, Big Sweet enjoyed playing cards with the men on the job. Hoodoo, a spiritual belief and practice that was derived from pre-Christian African traditions, provided an alternative value system that allowed women like Big Sweet to preserve their bodily and psychological integrity.

Janie Crawford, the protagonist of *Their Eyes Were Watching God*, begins with the meekness of Delia Jones and ends with the fierce will to save herself that one associates with Big Sweet. Although she is not a hoodoo initiate, Janie learns to listen to storms and to speak wisely. Of course, she learns to "change her own words" as well. The shy sixteen-year-old that readers meet in the early chapters of the novel has a gift for metaphor, yet lacks the confidence to speak her adorned language aloud. In an often-cited scene Janie lies under a pear tree and experiences an awakening that is both sexual and spiritual:

She was stretched on her back beneath the pear tree soaking in
the alto chant of the visiting bees, the gold of the sun and the
panting breath of the breeze when the inaudible voice of it all
came to her. She saw a dust-bearing bee sink into the sanctum of a
bloom; the thousand sister-calyxes arch to meet the love embrace
and the ecstatic shiver of the tree from root to tiniest branch
creaming in every blossom and frothing with delight. So this was a
marriage!

Janie's revelation is rendered lyrically in language that is also
frankly sexual. Sexuality was a vexed issue for women writers,
aware as they were of the licentious stereotypes of black women
that were pervasive in early-twentieth-century America. Hurston
was undaunted. She took a trite figure—the birds and the bees—
with which her protagonist would have been familiar, and adorns
it with the profusion of metaphor and simile that she identified as
characteristic of Negro expression. The novel gives the actual
words here to the narrator, who uses them to convey Janie's
thoughts.

When she tries to articulate her idea of marriage, Janie finds that
her stumbling words prove no match for the eloquence of her
grandmother, Nanny. Nanny is a preacher without a pulpit, who
fuses the language of the King James Bible with domestic
metaphors and black vernacular speech. This former slave
narrates her life to her granddaughter. After being sexually
exploited by her master, Nanny recounts, "Freedom found me wid
a baby daughter in mah arms, so Ah said Ah'd take a broom and a
cook-pot and throw up a highway through de wilderness for her."
Nanny's hopes for her daughter are dashed, but she has a dream
and a text for Janie's life. She wants her to escape the hard labor
that has defined her life and that of women like her who have been
treated as the "mules" of the world. Nannie wants Janie to live like
the white women for whom Nanny has worked. She has a plan
and uses emotional blackmail to achieve it. "Put me down, easy,
Janie. I'm a cracked plate," she implores her granddaughter, who

accedes to her command and marries a farmer aptly named Logan Killicks.

Initially, Janie has no words for her second husband, Joe Starks, either. "Cityfied and stylish," Joe offers Janie what seem to be new possibilities. He courts her in rhymes, and she reciprocates by giving him the pet name "Jody." Enterprising and ambitious, he takes her to Eatonville, where he challenges the people to incorporate the town, and they in turn elect him mayor. "A whirlwind among breezes," he stuns the people with his energy: soon he is storekeeper and postmaster as well as mayor. He even orders the town's first street lamp, and the people improvise a ceremony to honor the occasion. Janie soon realizes that she is to be a silent partner in Joe's enterprises. He is quick to inform the crowd that gathers for his election as mayor of the town that his wife knows nothing about speechmaking. He later orders her off the store porch when storytelling sessions are in progress; she is not allowed to participate in the rituals of the town. Joe wants her to be a decoration—young, pretty, and mute.

Yet Janie sustains a rich interior life and continues to invent metaphors to explore it: "She stood there until something fell off the shelf inside her. Then she went inside there to see what it was. It was her image of Jody tumbled down and shattered....She had an inside and an outside now and suddenly she knew how not to mix them." Denied the right to speak in public, Janie seizes the right to keep silent in private. Her ability to keep her inside feelings to herself allows her to survive what would otherwise be an intolerable situation. She also owns the responsibility for having made a bad choice, that of having been seduced by Joe's "big voice" and by her need to escape the man who was killing her dreams. She has kept the dreams alive and now decides that she is saving them for another man. After two decades of marriage, Janie gains the will to "talk back" to her husband. Her sharp words figuratively kill him.

With her third husband, a blues troubadour named Tea Cake, who is twenty years her junior, Janie learns to express herself. Tea Cake lacks material things, a guitar is his only possession, but his cultural knowledge is profound. He guides Janie into a greater understanding of rural southern black culture so much so that their romance is rich in its bywords. He tells Janie, "Nobody else on earth kin hold uh candle tuh you, baby. You got de keys to de kingdom." She tells a friend, "Dis ain't no business proposition, and no race after property and titles. Dis is uh love game."

Their Eyes Were Watching God is a love story, yet it is more than that. It represents a quest for selfhood, one of the oldest plots in literature, if one that rarely featured a female protagonist. The characters are black and southern, and the novel's language is rooted in the adorned speech of rural black southerners. The novel's major achievement is its treatment both of the characters and of the language with a stunning originality and seriousness.

Black vernacular speech allowed Hurston and Hughes, Toomer, Weldon, Johnson, and Brown to experiment with language and to make it new, as Ezra Pound was urging white modernists to do. Black modernists recognized the "new" in the old oral traditions that had never been part of literature. Weldon Johnson and Hurston remembered the sermons they had heard as children; the preachers' poetry sparked the writers' literary imaginations as adults. For Weldon Johnson that meant fashioning "sermons in verse" that were inspired by the art of unlettered preachers. Hurston not only transcribed sermons that she collected in the field, she drew on them for the narrative of Nanny, who belonged to a generation of women for whom the pulpit was proscribed. Spirituals echo through this writing: they inform the poetry of Toomer's *Cane* as well as the fiction of Hughes and Hurston. Toomer combined language drawn from southern black speech and the techniques of modernist fiction and poetry. *Cane* includes a poem based on a work song, as well an imagist poem.

Rather than the sonnet or the villanelle, Hughes and Brown turned to the blues for their poetry, which gave them models of meter, rhyme scheme, and structure. The blues offered a worldview as well, one that accepted death and trouble as facts of life that could not be transcended, but could be survived. Although it partook of a philosophy that could be called stoic, this worldview was, as the title of Hughes's novel, *Not Without Laughter*, inscribed. The rhythm of the blues was danceable survival music.

Not everyone thought the blues poetry was real poetry. To some, folk sermons were more the stuff of comedy than literary art. Ironically, preacher poets like those who inspired Weldon Johnson's *God's Trombones* kept the volume in print. For his part, Hughes sustained an audience by the force of his will; for decades he packed books to sell as he toured the country. Some readers found what Hurston called "Negro idiom" anything but beautiful and difficult to decipher. Brown and Hurston published their major works after the vogue had ended, and then the audience for any black writing was extremely small. In terms of style and subject, however, their work definitely belongs to the Harlem Renaissance. Two generations would pass, but these writers, who explored the "strong roots" of African American folklore, would eventually be embraced. Zora Neale Hurston is arguably now the most widely read author of her generation.

The example of Louis Armstrong illuminates the similar but different creative opportunities and obstacles available to the writers of the Harlem Renaissance and their musical contemporaries. Like the writers of the period, Armstrong's art is rooted in the expressive traditions of black southerners. No writer reached a fraction of the working-class black audience, North and South, who regularly danced to Armstrong's records. He won their approval long before his genius was recognized by the world. It was clear to all that Armstrong set the standard for the music he created.

Armstrong joined the Great Migration in 1922; like many Louisianans, his destination was Chicago rather than New York. In his native New Orleans, he was already renowned for his blues performances, having heard blues songs all his life. After he learned to play the cornet at the New Orleans Home for Colored Waifs, he made blues part of his repertoire. He arrived in Chicago in August 1922 and joined King Oliver's Creole Jazz Band, which played at the Lincoln Gardens, a cavernous club catering to a black clientele. Surrounded as he was by the music and cuisine of New Orleans, Armstrong was very much at home in Chicago. Audiences loved him. His facility with his instrument threatened to overshadow the ailing King Oliver, who insisted that Armstrong play with less volume and lower in range, but he was noticed nevertheless as his skill at improvisation and his technical mastery were singular. Armstrong soon struck out on his own. His sessions with blues queens Ma Rainey and Bessie Smith were further proof of his deep affinity for blues.

Armstrong's recordings with the "Hot Five," including Kid Ory on trombone, Johnny Dodds on clarinet, and Johnny St. Cyr on banjo, all from New Orleans, along with his wife Lil Hardin on piano, became jazz landmarks. Many of Armstrong's early records had "blues" somewhere in the title: "Canal Street Blues," Chimes Blues," and "Potato Head Blues," as well as several versions of W. C. Handy's classic, "St. Louis Blues," especially one recorded with Bessie Smith. Trained in New Orleans to play by ear, Armstrong learned musical notation in Chicago and even copyrighted songs like "Cornet Chop Suey Blues," a tune that could have been created only in the North; it paid tribute to the Chinese food popular among blacks on Chicago's South Side. Like his fellow migrants, Armstrong was able to blend the new aspects of northern life with the traditions he brought with him from the South.

As a musician, Armstrong battled with record companies, negotiated relationships with club owners and gangsters—Al Capone was a regular at his Chicago performances—and with white musicians who came to listen and to mimic his techniques, as well as the black musicians who studied his records until they could play his solos note-for-note. In addition to the indignities of segregation, Armstrong suffered the psychological indignity of knowing that Paul Whiteman, a white musician, was the acknowledged "King of Jazz" in the 1920s. Nonetheless, Armstrong and his fans knew better.

Armstrong's prodigious talent, his strong roots in the blues, apprenticeship to King Oliver, and years of discipline and practice culminated in Armstrong's 1928 masterpiece "West End Blues." Although written by King Oliver, with lyrics by Clarence Williams, Armstrong's interpretation and performance made the tune a classic. His band featured Fred Robinson on trombone, Jimmy Strong on clarinet, Mancy Cara on banjo, Zutty Singleton on drums, and Earl "Fatha" Hines on piano. The title refers to a neighborhood in New Orleans, which indicates Armstrong's strong sense of connection to his home place. The trumpet cadenzas that open and close the piece are irrefutable evidence of Armstrong's virtuosity. The twelve-bar blues in which Armstrong uses his voice as an instrument is one of the earliest examples of scat singing where he vocalizes nonverbal syllables. Armstrong fairly invented scat, a technique that Billie Holiday and Ella Fitzgerald and others would embellish. It intensifies the feeling in "West End Blues," conveying the emotional power of the blues, even as the high notes he hits and holds on the trumpet set a new bar for jazz musicians. In Armstrong's performance, the strong roots of the blues are the foundation of jazz, the quintessential music of modernism.

Epilogue: Beyond Harlem

Many Renaissance writers did not make Harlem their home. Anne Spencer lived in Lynchburg, Virginia, and offered hospitality to black northerners who were traveling south. Given the Jim Crow laws that denied them public accommodations, W. E .B. Du Bois, James Weldon Johnson, and Alain Locke stopped over with Spencer's family. They appreciated her hospitality, enjoyed her garden (now a site on the National Register of Historic Places), and encouraged her writing. Claude McKay (fig. 10) spent more time in Marseilles and Morocco than in Harlem, and Zora Neale Hurston lived mainly on the road. Their writings chart their travels. In *Banjo, A Story Without a Plot* and in *Their Eyes Were Watching God*, both McKay and Hurston represented communities that were a long way from Lenox Avenue; the writer and painter Gwendolyn Bennett's Paris sojourn inspired a short story set in Montmartre, the neighborhood in which a score of black American veterans relocated after World War I; the clubs they opened there established jazz as an international music. Paris was also the site for encounters among West African, Caribbean, and Negro American intellectuals, who exchanged political and literary philosophies. In their travels as well as their writings, New Negro artists and intellectuals brought the Renaissance beyond Harlem. They also encountered peers who were themselves at work on the challenge of being black in the modern world.

10. While Claude McKay wrote poems, fiction, and essays celebrating 1920s Harlem, he spent most of the decade outside of the United States. This undated photograph shows him in Paris, standing in front of one of the iconic bookstands on the Left Bank.

Sterling Brown despised Harlem, which he called "the show window, the cashier's till" of the New Negro Movement; in his view, the vogue for the Negro undermined the struggle for an honest racial identity. He hated the patronage that supported many artists and was keenly conscious of the commodification of Negro culture in the nightclubs of Harlem. His harshly satiric poem, "Cabaret," is set in a nightclub with a faux plantation décor. Three voices speak: a voice in the present describes the clientele and the chorus line, a voice that speaks from the past conjures up slave auctions and flooded levees, and a voice sings the folk song, "Muddy Water." The implication that the cabaret was as much a site of the exploitation of black bodies as the plantation is unmistakable.

Many black artists who lived in Harlem traveled extensively. Evidently, they found the air freer to breathe abroad. Like their white compatriots, they considered mainstream American culture philistine. Several New Negro intellectuals had studied in Europe and were eager to return. Like painters across Europe and the United States, Negro artists were eager to study in the City of Light. These black visual artists joined painters from Europe and the United States. Yet they had particular reasons to flee Harlem, if only temporarily.

Helga Crane, the fictional protagonist of Nella Larsen's 1929 novel, *Quicksand*, tries hard to convince herself that "Harlem is enough." The novel, however, argues otherwise. For all its art and glamour, Harlem was a segregated section of a segregated city. It was the manufactured danger of racial intermingling at the so-called black-and-tan cabarets and at Van Vechten's parties that made those venues stand out. Even in New York City, Negroes lived in one world and whites in another. Helga eventually finds the constrictions of race unbearable and escapes to Copenhagen. There she traverses the entire city with ease; she visits shops and theaters with no fear that she might be asked to leave. Initially, she basks in the attention of the Danes, who find her beautiful and exotic. Ultimately, however, she realizes that their admiration is tainted with primitivist myths. In a key scene, she cannot recognize herself in a portrait painted by a leading artist. He has projected onto the Chicago-born Helga his personal fantasies of African women. Helga returns to Harlem, then to the rural South, in search of a home she cannot find: Larsen's fictional journeys that the novel maps had real-life counterparts.

Paris had long been a city of refuge for Negro artists and intellectuals. Henry Ossawa Tanner, a pioneering painter who was interested mainly in religious subjects, moved to Paris permanently in 1894. He became a guide to New Negro artists when they arrived. During the Harlem Renaissance, the painters William Johnson and Archibald Motley, along with the sculptor Augusta Savage, followed Tanner's lead. Savage's efforts to do so became a cause célèbre. Born in Florida in 1892, she studied at New York City's Cooper Union from 1921 to 1924; in 1923 she won a fellowship to the Fontainebleau School of Fine Arts, but was later rejected when her American sponsors learned that she was black. W. E. B. Du Bois took up her cause but to no avail, and Jessie Fauset fictionalized Savage's struggle in a subplot of *Plum Bun*. In 1926 Savage won a fellowship to attend the Royal Academy of Fine Arts in Rome, which she had to decline because of inadequate funds. With a Rosenwald Foundation fellowship, she was finally able to study in Paris for three years, beginning in 1929. She went on to have a distinguished career as a sculptor and teacher.

Jessie Fauset was a frequent visitor to Paris; her first trip was to study at the Sorbonne shortly before World War I broke out. In an essay "Tracing Shadows," she described the fear, anticipation, and denial that defined the atmosphere in the summer of 1914. Thus, the shadows of the title become the portents of war. As in most essays, the emphasis is personal; it focuses on the persona's rite of passage against the backdrop of international events. Traveling with a group of women and men identified only by type (the Musician, Our Lady of Leisure, the Artist), the "I" of the essay is so enamored of the city ("Paris was for us and we were for Paris") that she is oblivious of the warnings imbedded in the conversations of the Parisians, mainly working class, whom she meets. When the mobilization begins, she and her friends have neither the cash nor the documents required for escape. For two weeks she lives through a "nightmare of sorrow and grief and pain" that will "mark" her forever. The tales of heroism she records celebrate the courage of men on their way to war as well as the courage of women who stay behind and add the work of the absent men to their usual labor. The reader comes to not only admire their heroism but also the perception of Fauset's persona to acknowledge it. Given the essay's thoroughgoing admiration for the French, it is not surprising that its author would return to Paris as often as she could.

On a visit in 1925, she told a reporter for the *Herald Tribune*, "I like Paris because I find something here, something of integrity, which I seem to have strangely lost in my own country." She added, "I like to live among people and surroundings where I am not always conscious of 'thou shall not.'" Although, she hastened to add, "I am colored and wish to be known as colored, . . . sometimes I have felt that my growth as a writer has been hampered in my own country. And so—but only temporarily—I have fled from it." She confided to friends that she had gotten a taste of cosmopolitan life in Paris, such as was off-limits to her even in New York. Nonetheless, Fauset was sensitive to slights. She remembered that Sylvia Beach, the proprietor of the English-language Shakespeare & Company bookstore and publisher of James Joyce's *Ulysses*, did not acknowledge Fauset's note of introduction. Fairly or not, Fauset took Beach's silence as an affront. For the most part, Fauset kept a safe distance from other members of the fabled American expatriate community—Gertrude Stein, Ernest Hemingway, Ezra Pound, and H. D. (Hilda Doolittle).

Langston Hughes had a wholly different Paris experience from either the expatriates or his mentor Fauset. He worked as a dishwasher at the *Le Grand Duc* nightclub in the heart of Montmartre, which Henri Toulouse-Lautrec memorialized in his paintings and lithographs of dancers and prostitutes. During the First World War, blacks had been relegated to menial tasks in the segregated army, but there was no Jim Crow in France. At the war's end, a few black soldiers decided to stay. They opened clubs that featured jazz musicians, notably Sidney Bechet, the premier soprano saxophonist and the only soloist who could hold his own on a stage with Louis Armstrong. For a time Josephine Baker reigned at *Chez Josephine*; Ada Smith, known as "Bricktop," ran a popular spot that she named after herself; *Le Grand Duc* was run by Eugene Bullard, a pilot and a prizefighter, who taught himself to play the drums in order to be part of the scene. Gwendolyn Bennett, who spent 1925 in Paris, was so taken with Bullard that she wrote a short story about him.

In "Wedding Day," Bennett's narrator describes Montmartre as "black Paris; the Rue Pigalle is its Seventh Avenue." The protagonist, Paul Watson, is an American prizefighter who is imprisoned for killing a white American who calls him "nigger." Freed by the war in which he fought valiantly, Watson returns to Paris. He has no patience with his white countrymen, and his friends are therefore surprised when he falls in love with a white American prostitute. He proposes, but on the day of their nuptials, she sends a letter explaining that she cannot go through with the marriage: she cannot marry a "nigger." Bennett was not the only American Negro to report that racism was part of the baggage white Americans brought to France. She did not, however, emphasize the prejudice that was already there. That was left to Claude McKay.

While he enjoyed the freedom of Paris, McKay found himself unable to work there. He preferred Marseilles, where he encountered a community of West African and Caribbean sailors and dockworkers, many of whom had fought for France during the war. The diasporic community fired McKay's imagination. *Banjo:*

A Story Without a Plot (1929) is a picaresque novel that features the protagonist Lincoln Agrippa Daily, an American Negro, whose nickname "Banjo" is a tribute to his command of the instrument. Banjo has slipped the bonds of oppression by making a life for himself in the *vieux port* of Marseilles, or, as the novel's characters prefer, the Ditch. The setting is rife with prostitution and petty crime. Like Jake in *Home to Harlem*, Banjo lives by his wits; he fortifies himself with wine and with the music he continually makes. The novel also reintroduces Ray, the Haitian intellectual, from *Home to Harlem*, who joins Banjo in this new adventure.

The interactions among the characters illuminate the continuities and discontinuities in their experiences across the diaspora. Almost every character addresses what the novel terms "the race question." Each is eloquent in his own way, giving lie to the belief that only educated people could analyze the situation they found themselves in. Their analyses are both global, as characters reflect on the histories of their homelands, and local, as they comment on the conflicts among the denizens of the Ditch and the conflicts between them and the French. Dispossession and colonialization are common conditions, yet they do not produce a common consciousness. Barriers of language and culture as well as individual points of view undermine the potential for unity. Vagabonds and roustabouts, the characters do not believe in the possibility of social change. Yet, the characters not only understand their marginal status as a consequence of history and oppression, they refuse to bend to the will of their colonizers. The novel suggests that these in themselves are acts of protest.

McKay had explored a similar thematic in *Home to Harlem*; the transnational community of characters in *Banjo* foregrounds the political implications of their stance. West African and Afro-Caribbean intellectuals, working and studying in Paris, were quick to embrace *Banjo* and its author. The poet Léopold Senghor came to Paris from French West Africa, enrolled at the Sorbonne in 1928, and eventually returned to Africa to become the first president of the independent nation of Senegal. In Paris he met the Martinique-born Aimé Césaire, a fellow student; fulfilling the titular prophecy of Césaire's signature volume, *Cahier d'un retour au pays natal* (*Notebook of Return to a Native Land*), Césaire became the long-serving mayor of Fort-de-France, the capital of Martinique. Léon Damas was born in French Guiana and met Césaire in Martinique. When he too came as a student to Paris, he reunited with Césaire and met Senghor. The three men are credited with developing the concept of *Négritude* that attempted to identify distinctive African cultural characteristics, aesthetics, and values as part of what might be understood as an act of cultural decolonization. They rightly saw their project as analogous to that of McKay and Hughes, whose books were quickly translated into French. All were concerned with envisioning a world in which people of African descent were free, politically and culturally. All wanted to incorporate the past expressive traditions of their people into art that would speak to the demands of the modern world.

The next generation of Negro writers in the United States was not impressed. Ralph Ellison referred dismissively to the "so-called renaissance." Richard Wright's response was scathing. "Generally speaking," he averred in 1937, "Negro writing in the past has been confined to humble novels, poems, and plays, prim and decorous ambassadors who went a-begging to white America." In its place, he offered a "Blueprint for Negro Writing," first published in the journal *New Challenge* (1937), which would show his contemporaries how to achieve the political ends that his precursors, in his view, had failed even to pursue. Most the books published during the Harlem Renaissance went out of print.

In the 1960s as black writers envisioned a "Black Arts Movement" that would liberate their voices, they rediscovered the movement of the 1920s. Both movements centered issues of identity and race, the role of the artist in the political struggle, and the meaning of Africa to blacks in the United States. Writers in both decades experimented with the rhythms of jazz and the distinctive patterns of African American English vernacular speech. Neither movement was strictly literary; both encompassed the visual and performing arts. Recognizing the similarity in the challenges they faced, black artists and their audiences in the 1960s rediscovered the Harlem Renaissance. Although they would find new answers to the old questions, they first needed to read their precursors' writings for themselves.

By the end of the decade new editions of Johnson's *The Book of American Negro Poetry* and Locke's *The New Negro* were available, followed by novels and facsimile editions of little magazines. Scholars wrote intellectual and social histories, biographies, and literary criticism. Many writers found inspiration in forgotten texts: Denzy Senna in *Passing*, Alice Walker in *Their Eyes Were Watching God*, and a host of poets in *Cane*. Of course, some writers did not need to be rediscovered because they had never been lost. Langston Hughes is foremost among these ; tellingly, his poems had long been embraced by ordinary readers, even as critics neglected them.

Readers can now collect an entire library of books from and about the Harlem Renaissance. The paintings and sculpture of the period are now part of the collections of major museums. Blues and jazz, the music that many New Negro critics dismissed, became the foundation for twentieth-century American music. The legacies of the Harlem Renaissance are all around us.

References

Chapter 1: "When the Negro was in vogue"

Langston Hughes, *The Big Sea* (New York: Hill and Wang, 1940), 228.

Rudolph Fisher, "The Caucasian Storms Harlem," *American Mercury* 11 (August 1927), 393–98.

Alain Locke, "The New Negro," in *The New Negro*, ed. Alain Locke (New York: Albert and Charles Boni, 1925; repr., New York: Atheneum, 1992), 6.

Hughes, *Big Sea*, 62, 228.

Langston Hughes, "The Weary Blues," in *The Collected Poems of Langston Hughes*, ed. Arnold Rampersad with David Roessel (1925; New York: Knopf, 1994), 50.

Claude McKay, *A Long Way From Home* (New York: Lee Furman, 1937; repr., New Brunswick, NJ: Rutgers University Press, 2007), 30.

Jean Toomer quoted in Alain Locke, "New Youth Speaks," in Locke, *New Negro*, 51.

Jessie Fauset to Jean Toomer, February 17, 1922, Jean Toomer Collection, Fisk University Archives.

Zora Neale Hurston, *Dust Tracks on a Road*, in *Zora Neale Hurston: Folklore, Memoir and other Writings*, ed. Cheryl A. Wall (Philadelphia: J. B. Lippincott, 1942; repr., New York: Library of America, 1995), 688.

Phyllis Rose, *Jazz Cleopatra: Josephine Baker in Her Time* (New York: Doubleday, 1989), 25, 31.

Josephine Baker quoted in Lynn Haney, *Naked at the Feast: A Biography of Josephine Baker* (New York: Dodd, Mead, 1981), 88.

Arthur Schomburg, "The Negro Digs Up His Past" in Locke, *New Negro*, 231.

Chapter 2: Inventing new selves

Alain Locke, Introduction, in Locke, *New Negro*, xxv.

Claude McKay, "If We Must Die," in *Collected Poems of Claude McKay*, ed. William Maxwell (1920; Urbana: University of Illinois Press, 2004), 177.

Locke, "New Negro," 15.

Countee Cullen, "From the Dark Tower," in *My Soul's High Song: The Collected Writings of Countee Cullen*, ed. Gerald Early (New York: Harper and Brothers, 1927; New York: Anchor Books, 1991), 139.

"Negro Wins Prize in Poetry Contest" (includes quotation from Countee Cullen), *New York Times*, December 2, 1923.

Hughes, "I, Too," in Rampersad, *Collected Poems of Langston Hughes*, 46.

James Van Der Zee, Owen Dodson, and Camille Billops, *The Harlem Book of the Dead* (New York: Morgan and Morgan, 1978), 43.

Van Der Zee, *Harlem Book of the Dead*, 83.

Elise Johnson McDougald, "The Task of Negro Womanhood," in Locke, *New Negro*, 369–70.

Marita Bonner, "On Being Young–a Woman–and Colored," *Crisis* (June 1925): 63–65, repr. in *Frye Street and Environs*, ed. Joyce Flynn and Joyce Occomy Stricklin (Boston: Beacon Press, 1987), 5, 7.

Georgia Douglas Johnson, "Wishes," *Crisis* (April 1927): 49.

Jessie Fauset, *Plum Bun, A Novel Without a Moral* (New York: Frederick A. Stokes, 1928); repr., Boston: Beacon Press, 1990), 145.

Nella Larsen, *Passing* (New York: Alfred A. Knopf, 1929); repr., New Brunswick, NJ: Rutgers University Press, 1986), 159; 177.

Bessie Smith, "Young Woman's Blues." Recorded October 26, 1926, with Joe Smith, cornet; Buster Bailey, clarinet; Fletcher Henderson, piano; and Bessie Smith, vocals. Columbia 14179–D.

Ma Rainey, "Prove It On Me." June 1928. Ma Rainey and the Tub Jug Band. Paramount 12668.

Hughes, "The Negro Artist and the Racial Mountain," *Nation*, June 23, 1926, 692–94.

Chapter 3: Harlem: City of dreams

Countee Cullen, "Harlem Wine," in *Color* (New York: Harper and Brothers, 1925), 13.

James Weldon Johnson, "Harlem: the Culture Capital," in Locke, *New Negro*, 301.

Richard Bruce Nugent, Memoir, unpub., Schomburg Center for Research in Black Culture, np.

Adam Clayton Powell Sr., quoted in Jervis Anderson, *This Is Harlem* (New York: Farrar, Straus and Giroux, 1982), 61.

Langston Hughes, *Big Sea*, 240.

Arna Bontemps, "The Awakening: A Memoir," in *The Harlem Renaissance Remembered*, ed. Arna Bontemps (New York: Dodd, Mead, 1972), 15.

Zora Neale Hurston, *Dust Tracks on a Road*, in Wall, *Zora Neale Hurston*, 682.

Jessie Fauset to Jean Toomer, February 17, 1922, Jean Toomer Collection, Fisk University Archives.

Jessie Fauset, "Our Book Shelf," review of *The Weary Blues* by Langston Hughes, *Crisis* (March 1926): 239.

Langston Hughes, *Big Sea*, 247.

Claude McKay, *Long Way from Home*, 112.

Rudolph Fisher, *The Walls of Jericho* (New York: Alfred A. Knopf, 1928), repr., New York: Arno Press, 1969), 79.

Zora Neale Hurston, "A Glossary of Harlem Slang," *American Mercury* 45 (July 1942): 94–96.

Rudolph Fisher, "The City of Refuge" in Locke, *New Negro*, 58, 74.

Claude McKay, "The Tropics in New York," in Maxwell, ed. *Collected Poems* (1920; Urbana: University of Illinois Press, 2004), 154.

Claude McKay, *Long Way from Home*, 96.

Claude McKay, *Home to Harlem* (New York: Harper and Brothers, 1928); repr., Boston: Northeastern University Press, 1987), 153, 93.

W. E. B. Du Bois, "Two Novels," review of *Home to Harlem* by Claude McKay and *Quicksand* by Nella Larsen, *Crisis* (June 1928): 202.

Claude McKay to James Weldon Johnson, April 30 1928, James Weldon Johnson Memorial Collection of African American Arts and Letters, Beinecke Rare Book and Manuscript Library, Yale University.

Langston Hughes, *Big Sea*, 274.

Helene Johnson, "Sonnet to a Negro in Harlem" in *Caroling Dusk: An Anthology of Verse by Negro Poets*, ed. Countee Cullen (New York: Harper and Brothers, 1927), 217.

Amy Jacques-Garvey, ed., *Philosophy and Opinions of Marcus Garvey* (New York: Athenaeum, 1969), 81, 5, 77.

Amy Jacques-Garvey, *Philosophy and Opinions*, 426.

Amy Jacques-Garvey, *Philosophy and Opinions*, 10.

W. E. B. Du Bois, "A Lunatic or a Traitor," *Crisis* (May 1924): 8–9.

E. David Cronon, *Black Moses: The Story of Marcus Garvey and the Universal Negro Improvement Association* (Madison: University of Wisconsin Press, 1969), 60.

W. E. B. Du Bois, "The Negro Mind Reaches Out," in Locke, *New Negro*, 386, 406.

Jessie Fauset, "Impressions of the Pan African Congress," *Crisis* (November 1921): 17–18.

Jessie Fauset, "No End of Books," review of *Batouala* by René Maran, *Crisis* (March 1922): 208–10.

Jessie Fauset to Joel Spingarn, January 25, 1922, Joel Spingarn Collection, New York Public Library.

Jessie Fauset, "Dark Algiers the White," *Crisis* (April 1925): 244–58; (May 1925): 16–22.

Countee Cullen, "Fruit of the Flower," in Early, *My Soul's High Song*, 95.

Alain Locke, "The Legacy of the Ancestral Arts," in Locke, *New Negro*, 254, 260, 256.

Nathan Huggins, *Harlem Renaissance* (New York: Oxford University Press, 1971), 177.

Langston Hughes, "The Negro Speaks of Rivers," in Rampersad, *Collected Poems*, 23.

Langston Hughes, "Afro-American Fragment," in Rampersad, *Collected Poems*, 129.

Chapter 5: "Strong roots sink down"

Zora Neale Hurston, *Dust Tracks*, in Wall, *Zora Neale Hurston*, 605.

James Weldon Johnson, Preface, *The Book of American Negro Poetry*, 2nd ed. (New York: Harcourt, Brace, 1931); repr., (1969), 41, 4.

James Weldon Johnson, *God's Trombones: Seven Negro Sermons in Verse* (New York: Viking Press, 1927), 5.

Johnson, "The Creation," *God's Trombones*, 18.

W. E. B. Du Bois, *The Souls of Black Folk* (Chicago: A. C. McClurg, 1903; repr., New York: Penguin, 1989), 205, 211.

Alain Locke, "The Negro Spirituals," in Locke, *New Negro*, 206.

Paul Robeson, quoted in Martin Duberman, *Paul Robeson* (New York: Alfred Knopf, 1988), 81.

Zora Neale Hurston, "Spirituals and Neo-Spirituals," in Wall, *Zora Neale Hurston*, 870.

Jean Toomer, *Cane* (New York: Boni and Liveright,1923); repr., New York: Liveright, 2011), 18.

Jean Toomer, *Cane*, 3, 8, 25.

Langston Hughes, "Young Gal Blues," in Rampersad, *Collected Poems*, 123.

Sterling Brown, "Ma Rainey," in *The Collected Poems of Sterling A. Brown*, ed. Michael S. Harper (New York: Harcourt Brace, 1932; repr., New York: Harper and Row, 1980), 62–64.

Sterling Brown, "Strong Men," in Harper, *Collected Poems*, 51–53.

Zora Neale Hurston, *Dust Tracks*, in Wall, *Zora Neale Hurston*, 601.

Zora Neale Hurston, *Mules and Men*, in Wall, *Zora Neale Hurston*, 10.

Zora Neale Hurston, "Characteristics of Negro Expression," in Wall, *Zora Neale Hurston*, 830–32.

Zora Neale Hurston, "Spirituals and Neo-Spirituals," in Wall, *Zora Neale Hurston*, 873.

Zora Neale Hurston, "Characteristics of Negro Expression," in Wall, *Zora Neale Hurston*, 834.

Zora Neale Hurston, *Their Eyes Were Watching God* (Philadelphia: J. P. Lippincott,1937); repr., New York: HarperCollins, 1990), 10–11.

Zora Neale Hurston, *Their Eyes*, 15, 67–68. 104, 108.

Epilogue: Beyond Harlem

Sterling Brown, "The New Negro in Literature, 1925–1955," in *A Son's Return: Selected Essays of Sterling Brown*, ed. Mark Sanders (Boston: Northeastern University Press, 1996), 184–205.

Jessie Fauset, "Tracing Shadows," *Crisis* (September 1915): 247–51.

Jessie Fauset, quoted in *Paris Tribune*, February 1, 1923.

Richard Wright, "Blueprint for Negro Writing," *New Challenge 2* (1937): 53–65; repr. in *African American Literary Theory*, ed. Winston Napier (1937; New York: NYU Press, 2000), 45.

Gwendolyn Bennett, "Wedding Day," *Fire!!*, 1926, 25–28.

Further reading

From the Harlem Renaissance

Bonner, Marita. *Frye Street and Environs: The Collected Works of Marita Bonner*. Boston: Beacon Press, 1987.

Bontemps, Arna. *Black Thunder: Gabriel's Revolt: Virginia 1800*. New York: Macmillan, 1936. Reprinted with introduction by Arnold Rampersad. Boston: Beacon Press, 1992.

Bontemps, Arna. *God Sends Sunday: A Novel*. First published 1931 by New York: Harcourt, Brace and Co., 1931. Reprint, New York: Washington Square Press, 2005.

Brown, Sterling. *The Collected Poems of Sterling A. Brown*. Edited by Michael S. Harper. New York: Harper and Row, 1980.

Campbell, Mary S. *Harlem Renaissance: Art of Black America*. New York: Harry Abrams, 1987.

Gerald Early, ed. *My Soul's High Song: The Collected Writings of Countee Cullen*. New York: Anchor Books, 1991.

Fauset, Jessie. *Plum Bun*. 1928. Reprint, Boston: Beacon Press, 1990.

Hughes, Langston. *The Big Sea*. New York: Hill and Wang, 1940.

Hughes, Langston. *Not Without Laughter*. 1930. Reprint, New York: Barnes and Noble, 1995.

Hurston, Zora Neale. *Their Eyes Were Watching God*. 1937. Reprint, New York: HarperCollins, 1991.

Johnson, James Weldon. *The Autobiography of an Ex-Colored Man*. 1927, 1912. Reprint, New York: Penguin, 1990.

Johnson, James Weldon, ed. *The Book of American Negro Poetry*. 1931, 1922. Reprint, New York: Harcourt, 1969.

Johnson, James Weldon. *God's Trombones*. 1927. Reprint, New York: Penguin, 2008.

Larsen, Nella. *Quicksand* (1928) and *Passing* (1929). New Brunswick, NJ: Rutgers University Press. 1996.

Locke, Alain, ed. *The New Negro*. 1925. Reprint, New York: Athenaeum, 1991.

McKay, Claude. *Banjo*. 1929. Reprint, London: Serpent Tail's Press, 2008.

McKay, Claude. *Home to Harlem*. 1928. Reprint, Boston: Northeastern University Press, 1987.

McKay, Claude. *A Long Way from Home*. 1937. Reprint, New Brunswick, NJ: Rutgers University Press, 2007.

Powell, Richard, ed. *Archibald Motley: Jazz Age Modernist*. Durham, NC: Masher Museum of Art at Duke University, 2014.

Rampersad, Arnold, with David Roessel, eds. *The Collected Poems of Langston Hughes*. New York: Knopf, 1994.

Thurman, Wallace. *The Blacker the Berry*. 1929. Reprint, New York: Dover Editions, 2008.

Thurman, Wallace, *Infants of the Spring*. 1932. Reprint, New York: Dover Editions, 2013.

Toomer, Jean. *Cane*. 1923. Reprint, New York: Liveright, 2011.

Van Der Zee, James, Owen Dodson, and Camille Billops. *The Harlem Book of the Dead*. New York: Morgan and Morgan, 1978.

Wall, Cheryl A., ed. *Zora Neale Hurston: Folklore, Memoirs, and other Writings*. New York: Library of America, 1995.

Wall, Cheryl A., ed. *Zora Neale Hurston: Novels and Stories*. New York: Library of America, 1995.

White, Walter. *Fire in the Flint*. 1924. Reprint, Athens: University of Georgia Press, 1996.

White, Walter. *Flight*. 1926. Reprint, Baton Rouge: Louisiana State University Press, 1998.

Anthologies

Gable, Craig, ed. *Ebony Rising: Short Fiction of the Greater Harlem Renaissance Era*. Bloomington: Indiana University Press, 2004.

Gates, Henry Louis Jr., and Gene Andrew Jarrett, eds. *The New Negro: Readings on Race, Representation, and African American Culture, 1892–1938*. Princeton: Princeton University Press, 2007.

Honey, Maureen, ed. *Shadowed Dreams: Women's Poetry of the Harlem Renaissance*. New Brunswick, NJ: Rutgers University Press, 1989.

Lewis, David Levering, ed. *The Portable Harlem Renaissance Reader*. New York: Penguin Classics, 1995.

Patton, Venetria K., and Maureen Honey, eds. *Double-Take: A Revisionist Harlem Renaissance Anthology*. New Brunswick, NJ: Rutgers University Press, 2001.

About the Harlem Renaissance

Anderson, Jervis. *This Was Harlem: A Cultural Portrait, 1900–1950*. New York: Farrar, Straus and Giroux, 1982.

Anderson, Paul Allen. *Deep River: Music and Memory in Harlem Renaissance Thought*. Durham, NC: Duke University Press, 2001.

Baker, Houston. *Modernism and the Harlem Renaissance*. Chicago: University of Chicago Press, 1987.

Baldwin, Davarian L., and Minkah Makalani. *Escape from New York: The New Negro Renaissance Beyond Harlem*. Minneapolis: University of Minnesota Press, 2013.

Brown, Jayna. *Babylon Girls: Black Women Performers and the Shaping of the Modern*. Durham, NC: Duke University Press, 2008.

Carroll, Anne Elizabeth. *Word, Image, and the New Negro: Representation and Identity in the Harlem Renaissance*. Bloomington: Indiana University Press, 2005.

Davis, Angela. *Blues Legacies and Black Feminism*. New York: Vintage, 1990.

Edwards, Brent Hayes. *The Practice of Diaspora: Literature, Translation, and the Rise of Black Internationalism*. Cambridge, MA: Harvard University Press, 2003.

Ewing, Adam. *The Age of Garvey: How a Jamaican Activist Created a Mass Movement and Changed Global Black Politics*. Princeton: Princeton University Press, 2014.

Huggins, Nathan. *Harlem Renaissance*. New York: Oxford University Press, 1971.

Hull, Gloria. *Color, Sex, and Poetry: Three Women Writers of the Harlem Renaissance*. Bloomington: Indiana University Press, 1987.

Hutchinson, George. *The Harlem Renaissance in Black and White*. Cambridge, MA: Harvard University Press, 1995.

Kirschke, Amy Helene. *Women Artists of the Harlem Renaissance*. Jackson: University Press of Mississippi, 2014.

Lewis, David Levering, ed. *When Harlem Was in Vogue*. New York: Alfred A. Knopf, 1981.

Massood, Paula J. *Making a Promised Land: Harlem in Twentieth-Century Photography and Film*. New Brunswick, NJ: Rutgers University Press, 2013.

Mitchell, Verner D., and Cynthia Davis. *Literary Sisters: Dorothy West and Her Circle, a Biography of the Harlem Renaissance*. New Brunswick, NJ: Rutgers University Press, 2011.

Nadell, Martha J. *Enter the New Negroes: Images of Race in American Culture*. Cambridge, MA: Harvard University Press, 2004.

Schwarz, A. B. Christa. *Gay Voices of the Harlem Renaissance*. Bloomington: Indiana University Press, 2003.

Sherrard-Johnson, Cherene. *Portraits of the New Negro Woman: Visual and Literary Culture in the Harlem Renaissance*. New Brunswick, NJ: Rutgers University Press, 2007.

Smethurst, James. *The African American Roots of Modernism: From Reconstruction to the Harlem Renaissance*. Chapel Hill: University of North Carolina Press, 2011.

Spencer, Jon Michael. *The New Negroes and Their Music: The Success of the Harlem Renaissance*. Knoxville: University of Tennessee Press, 1997.

Stovall, Tyler. *Paris Noir: African Americans in the City of Light*. New York: Houghton Mifflin, 1986.

Thaggert, Miriam. *Images of Black Modernism: Verbal and Visual Strategies of the Harlem Renaissance*. Amherst: University of Massachusetts Press, 2010.

Vogel, Shane. *The Scene of Harlem Cabaret: Race, Sexuality, Performance*. Chicago: University of Chicago Press, 2009.

Wall, Cheryl A. *Women of the Harlem Renaissance*. Bloomington: Indiana University Press, 1995.

Watson, Steven. *The Harlem Renaissance: Hub of African-American Culture, 1920–1930*. New York: Pantheon, 1995.

Willis-Braithwaite, Deborah, and Rodger Birt. *VanDerZee, Photographer, 1886–1983*. New York: Harry N. Abrams, 1993.

Text credits

We are grateful for permission to include the following copyright material in this book:

Brown, Sterling
From "Ma Rainey" and "Strong Men" from *The Collected Poems of Sterling Brown*, edited by Michael S. Harper. Reprinted by permission of the Estate of Sterling A. Brown.

Cullen, Countee
"Harlem Wine"
From "Fruit of the Flower"
From "Heritage" © Amistad Research Center

Hughes, Langston
"I, Too," "The Negro Speaks of Rivers," "Afro-American Fragment," "Young Gal's Blues," and "Hard Daddy," from *The Collected Poems of Langston Hughes* by Langston Hughes, edited by Arnold Rampersad with David Roessel, editor, copyright © 1994 by the Estate of Langston Hughes. Used by permission of Alfred A. Knopf, an imprint of the Knopf/Doubleday Publishing Group, a division of Penguin Random House LLC. All rights reserved. Additional rights by permission of Harold Ober Associates Incorporated.

Johnson, Helene
""Poem" and "Sonnet to a Negro in Harlem" used by permission of Abigail McGrath.

Text credits

Index